Praise for
Culture Clash 2: Managing the
Global High-Performance Team

"When it comes to cultural differences, most of us don't even know what we don't even know. *Culture Clash* not only reminds us of our blindness, but also offers a cure. Pick it up, read it, and see what we're missing!" **—Scott A. Snook**
Professor, Harvard Business School

"A great read—and you end up smarter as a result of it. Absolutely required reading for leaders who manage across cultures." **—Ali Velshi**
Chief Business Correspondent, CNN

"*Culture Clash 2* is worth real money for global companies. The productivity of large corporations is directly linked to culture—the more senior you are, the more you have got to pay attention to cross-cultural roadblocks. If you want to build or manage a global high-performance team, read this book and give it to everyone around you." **—Steve Baird**
Senior Management Advisor, UBS

"*Culture Clash 2* is a masterfully written and thoughtful book, of chief importance to both private and public managers. To marshal leadership across cultures, to exploit international opportunities and to build global citizenship are among the great challenges prevailing; this book provides an indispensable tutorial for confronting these challenges, including research insights, pragmatic tools and insightful as well as entertaining stories of authentic examples. " **—Dr. Sascha Spoun**
President, Leuphana Universität Lüneburg

"I wish I had had access to Zweifel's tools 35 years ago when I was starting out." **—Werner Brandmayr**
Former President and Managing Director,
ConocoPhillips Continental Holding GmbH

"I just wish *Culture Clash 2* had been available at the start of my personal globalization, it would have saved me a lot of time and pain. I would recommend this book as essential reading for any international manager." **—Dr. Martin Cross**
Former CEO, Novartis-Australia

"The lessons, labs, and the 'dos and taboos' give good input for daily exercise as long as the reader has the will to improve his or her communication abilities." **—Dr. Gerhard Goerres**
Chefarzt Radiologie, Bürgerspital Solothurn

"This is very much a message that boards of directors must understand if they are to lead their successful domestic business to become truly multinational organizations. Today, you need to build truly global governance—global teams committed to the organization's overarching objectives, but at the same time adaptive to local conditions and challenges. Tools like the Spidergraph will help you do that." **—John Hall**
Chief Executive Officer, Australian Institute of Company Directors

"As Japan's former chief diplomat, I have seen time and time again how small cross-cultural misunderstandings can spin out of control. We live in dangerous and turbulent times in international affairs, and we must do everything in our power to bridge cultural differences. Thomas Zweifel's book helps us do exactly that. It is an important and timely book, and it should be read by all those who are working not only to prevent culture clash, but for our common future as humanity." **—Hon. Koji Kakizawa**
Member, House of Representatives, Japan;
former Foreign Minister, Japan

"We use *Culture Clash 2* in our advanced leadership course. It is a great tool in building the skills the Army needs in the 21st century." **—Col. Joseph LeBoeuf**
Academy Professor, Director, Organizational Studies and Leadership,
Fuqua School of Business, Duke University

"As an ambassador and career diplomat, I observe and experience every day that one never quite achieves global citizenship—but one has to keep approaching it, keep bridging the cultures and find the common denominators of all civilizations and human beings. You have to "love" your negotiating partner and search for common ground, for common values, for what unites you, and take it as a basis to build a win-win situation. Thomas Zweifel's book gives you both the philosophy and the instruments. I commend *Culture Clash 2* to all those who must master the art of cross-cultural management. If you read it, you will get superior results in your negotiations." **—Ambassador Raymond Loretan**
Former Consul General of Switzerland to New York

"As CEO of a multinational company, I know that you have to understand another culture within the local cultural context. *Culture Clash 2* gave me new tools, a lot of food for thought and a real awareness for cultural issues in an easy-to-understand manner. Refreshing and great fun to read." **—Doris Marty-Albysser**
CEO, CLS Corporate Language Services AG

"I have worked for decades in the international finance community—Europe, North and Latin America, and Asia. Your advice, admonitions and secrets are priceless." **—Richard Murray**
Vice Chairman, LaProv Corporation

"Zweifel has distilled a wealth of intercultural theory, real-life case studies, and personal experience drawn from academia, the military, not-for-profits and the corporate world to produce a unique and fascinating read and an invaluable primer for both the neophyte and experienced international managers alike. As a cross-cultural practitioner, I can highly recommend this refreshing approach to understanding and managing the complexities of doing business across cultures." **—Georgina Teague**
Cross-cultural consultant, Australia

"... should be required reading for anyone who travels, or just for dealing with people of different cultures on our own home turf."
—Roseanne Schnoll, PhD, RD, CDN
Associate Professor, Department of Health and Nutrition Sciences,
Brooklyn College of CUNY

"*Culture Clash 2: Managing the Global High-Performance Team* is a fascinating and clearly written book that will greatly empower the managers of any global corporation or team. Thomas Zweifel's many years of experience working effectively in cultures all over the world has given him an uncanny and insightful access to the real and profound keys to success working cross-culturally, where a minefield of mistakes are often waiting to happen. His book is clear, concise and gets right down to the best nuggets available on this topic and he shares his insight with both wit and wisdom. A brilliant piece of work and highly relevant to today's global culture."
—Lynne Twist
President of The Turning Tide Coalition and
author of The Soul of Money

"*Culture Clash 2* is the perfect book for policymakers who have to integrate different cultures to fulfill their mandates. I recommend this book and its delightful stories and useful exercises to everyone in government, which is after all about harmonizing conflict and building consensus. This book really deserves support and success."
—Liszt Vieira
President of the Botanic Garden of Rio de Janeiro;
Former Minister of Environment in the State of Rio de Janeiro

". . . an inspiring read about getting it right. I've just finished reading another, similar book of over 300 pages and I think I got just as much good information from your 85 pages as the longer one. Well done."
—Deborah Wilson
Journalist, CBC Radio

"An excellent book . . . introducing you to the main issues of culture clash in the transnational business world. Most illustrative is Zweifel's "Global Leader Pyramid" showing you in one diagram the essence of culture and potential areas of conflict between Americans, Germans, Japanese, Indians, and Chinese, just to name a few of the most important nations. Every page is worth reading in this no-nonsense, no-bla-bla-bla book. Refreshingly concise and informative, contrasting many 600 page books."

—Dr. Peter Oertli
OEC Oertli Consulting

Culture Clash 2

Leading the Global High-Performance Team

THOMAS D. ZWEIFEL, PhD

SelectBooks, Inc.

New York

This edition published by SelectBooks, Inc.

For information address SelectBooks, Inc., New York, New York.

Second Edition

ISBN 978-1-59079-961-1

Library of Congress Cataloging-in-Publication Data

Zweifel, Thomas D., 1962-
  [Culture clash]
  Culture clash 2.0 : leading the global high-performance team / Thomas
D. Zweifel, Ph.D. — Second edition.
      pages cm
  Includes bibliographical references and index.
  Summary: "Consultant for an international management consulting firm
with thirty years of experience working on four continents with senior
executives at Fortune 500 companies and in governments, UN agencies,
and the military, presents a methodology of practical techniques for
bridging cultural differences to successfully manage business ventures in
the clash of cultures across the globe"—Provided by publisher.
  ISBN 978-1-59079-961-1 (pbk. : alk. paper)
1. International business enterprises—Management. 2. Leadership—
Cross-cultural studies. 3. Intercultural communication. 4. Globalization.
I. Title.
  HD62.4.Z85 2013
  658'.049—dc23
                                2013002689
            Manufactured in the United States of America
               10 9 8 7 6 5 4 3 2 1

To Gabrielle, Tina, and Hannah,
global citizens and travelers
who teach me tolerance

Contents

Acknowledgments *vii*

Foreword by Shideh S. Bina, Nathan Rosenberg, and
Michael Waldman *ix*

Preface *xv*

Chapter 1 **War Stories: The Ten Most Costly Sins When
Cultures Collide** *1*

Your War Stories? *7*
The Ten Most Costly Sins When Cultures Clash *13*
Your Culture Clash *28*

Chapter 2 **The New Leadership Landscape:
Global Is In, National Is Out** *31*

BRICS and Emerging Markets *34*
Communication, Transportation, Migration, Virtual Teams *37*
Americanization, Media, Social Media *42*
Multinational Organizations, International Organizations *44*

Chapter 3 **Leading through Language: What Do You Speak?** *49*

The Power if Cultural Mindsets *49*

Chapter 4 **Global Citizenship: A Core Competence** *59*

A Global Citizen's Mini-Briefing *60*
What's Your Cross-Cultural IQ? *66*

Chapter 5 **How to Avoid Cultural Clashes** *71*

Tool 1: Do's and Taboos of Global Citizenship *73*
Tool 2: Lawrence of Arabia—Quintessential Global Citizen *76*

Chapter 6 **Tools for Decoding Any Culture (Not Least Your Own)** *85*

Tool 3: Decoding Culture: From the Obvious to the Hidden *86*
Tool 4: The Global Integrator™: Eight Dimensions of Culture™ *92*
An Example: United States vs India *101*

Chapter 7   **Global Citizenship: Leading across Cultures** *105*

Tool 5: The Global Leader Pyramid™ *105*
Relationship *107*
Vision *108*
Strategy *109*
Action *111*
Lab: Sweeping Generalizations on Doing Business in Europe *112*

Chapter 8   **Cross-Cultural Strategy as an Asset for Innovation** *115*

From Multinational to *Metanational:* Searching for
    Innovation Globally *116*
Coke in China: What Went Wrong (and Right)? *121*
Pepsi: Repairing a Poisoned Reputation in India *122*
Best Practice: Building One Global Brand *126*

Chapter 9   **The Acid Test: Alliances and M&As** *127*

The GE Capital Model of Integration *133*

Chapter 10   **Making Global Meetings Work** *137*

Traditional vs. Virtual Meetings *138*
Before: Co-Creating the Agenda *141*
During: Keeping Things on Track *142*
After: Leveraging the Momentum *144*
Case: $40 Million Value-Add from Cross-Cultural Strategy
    and Leadership *145*

The Bottom Line . . . *147*

Appendix *149*

Notes *153*

Readings and Resources *158*

About the Author *161*

More Books by Thomas D. Zweifel *164*

Acknowledgments

This book is in large part a product of failures. Ever since my birth, I had the chance (or challenge, depending on how you see it) of living in many different cultures. I was born in Paris, moved to Switzerland at the tender age of five weeks with my parents in the back of their Simca convertible; grew up in Basel, which is in the triangle of France, Germany and Switzerland, learning that my culture and way of doing things was not the only one; moved to Berlin, then to Munich; moved to Bombay (now Mumbai), then New York, then San Francisco; then to London, then Tokyo, then back to New York; again to San Francisco, again to New York and finally (I hope) to Zurich. I have made so many mistakes in all these cultures—and this book is full of my confessions and war stories—that I can now consult clients on avoiding those mistakes and work effectively across borders and cultures. May I be forgiven for turning my own shortcomings into a lucrative business.

The other component of this book are the global strategies and best practices I was able to pick up from CEOs like Carlos Ghosn of Renault, Indra Nooyi of Pepsico or Jeffrey Immelt of GE, from leaders like Nelson Mandela and diplomats like former UN secretary general Javier Perez de Cuellar who I had the honor to work with in the 1990s, but also from road warriors and expats at all levels who face the global market, customers, suppliers, or alliance partners in far-flung regions. Since 2003, when the first edition of *Culture Clash* first saw the light of day, globalization has only grown and organizations of all stripes have recognized the need for effective cross-cultural management—not just as a HR skill, not merely as a nice-to-have or an afterthought, but as a strategic competence that can make or break a product and even a company. In the years since, countless practitioners have helped me refine and clarify the material; naming them all would take an entire book—and I mean that. Here are a few outstanding examples:

My readers, who use the knowledge and tools in my previous books to produce results across borders and who gave me many insightful war stories, constructive comments, and corrections.

Insigniam's partners and colleagues in the Americas, Europe and Asia, who assist clients in revealing and unhooking cultural blind-spots in the service of inventing new possibilities and implementing break-through performance. Swiss Consulting Group's and Manres' consultants, who stand for unleashing the human spirit. My leadership students at Columbia University, St. Gallen University, and Haute Ecole de Gestion Fribourg, who have challenged my thinking, help me keep up-to-date as a life-long learner, and make me wonder often why I get paid for teaching and why they have to pay tuition, when it should be the other way around.

Anne Nelson, my Columbia journalism teacher who first encouraged me to publish my writing despite my doubts (after all, Zweifel is German for "doubt") whether anyone would want to read my stuff. Shideh Bina, who enriched the book with her original thinking as well as priceless vignettes. Christine Flouton, Guillaume Pajeot, Ashley Tappan and other Insigniam consultants, who provided illustrative war stories of meanings lost in translation. Peter Guarco and Greg Trueblood, who fact-checked the book with a sharp eye for inaccuracies or dated material, and provided vital research. Nancy Sugihara and Molly Stern, whose first-class line-editing job made this a better book and in the process taught me new dimensions of the English language. Christian Dittus, my tireless agent at Paul & Peter Fritz Literary Agency, who continues to believe in my ideas and makes sure they find an audience.

Dr. Eva and the late Dr. Heinz Wicki-Schönberg, my parents and first role models in intercultural savvy (when I was born in Paris, it was customary to feed babies wine along with milk—how is that for cross-cultural training?) who braved their own culture clash when they moved from Basel to Sydney after my father's retirement; and above all my wife Gabrielle, who as a former flight attendant has been in more countries than I will ever visit and who is my teacher in Swiss-style diplomacy; and Tina and Hannah, *mes rayons de soleil* and emerging global citizens. Without hesitation they have embraced my quest as a writer, teacher and consultant amidst all the demands of family life, even when that quest took me away from home and to far-flung places. I am forever grateful for their love and support. Gabrielle in particular is the person that gives me the strength that underpins all that I do, and listens patiently to my peculiar ideas, weeding out the ones that are too wild and nurturing the others so they can see the light of day.

Of course none of these persons are responsible for my mistakes or exaggerations.

T.D.Z.
Zurich
March, 2013

Foreword

by Shideh S. Bina, Nathan O. Rosenberg, and Michael Waldman
Founding Partners, Insigniam

This exchange between an English-speaking traveller and a member of the hotel staff in a Far East hotel was recorded in the Far-East Economic Review about five years ago.[1]

Room Service: Morny. Rune-sore-bees.

Hotel Guest: Oh, sorry. I thought I dialed Room Service.

Room Service: Rye, rune-sore-bees. Morny. Djewish to odor sunteen?

Hotel Guest: Uh . . . yes. I'd like some bacon and eggs.

Room Service: Ow July den?

Hotel Guest: What?

Room Service: Aches. Ow July den? Pry, boy, pooch . . . ?

Hotel Guest: Oh, the eggs! How do I like them? Sorry. Scrambled please.

Room Service: Ow July dee baycome? Crease?

Hotel Guest: Crisp will be fine.

Room Service: Hokay. An Santos?

Hotel Guest: What?

Room Service: Santos. July Santos?

Hotel Guest: Ugh. I don't know . . . I don't think so.

Room Service: No. Judo one toes?

Hotel Guest:	Look, I feel really bad about this, but I don't know what "judo one toes" means. I'm sorry.
Room Service:	Toes! Toes! Why djew Don Juan toes? Ow bow eenglish mopping we bother?
Hotel Guest:	English muffin! I've got it! You were saying toast! Fine. An English muffin will be fine.
Room Service:	We bother?
Hotel Guest:	No. Just put the bother on the side.
Room Service:	Wad?
Hotel Guest:	I'm sorry. I meant butter. Butter on the side.
Room Service:	Copy?
Hotel Guest:	I feel terrible about this but. . .
Room Service:	Copy. Copy, tea, mill . . .
Hotel Guest:	Coffee! Yes, coffee please. And that's all.
Room Service:	One Minnie. Ass rune torino fee, strangle aches, crease baycome, tossy cenglish mopping we bother honey sigh, and copy. Rye?
Hotel Guest:	Whatever you say.
Room Service:	Hokay. Tendjewberrymud.
Hotel Guest:	You're welcome.

Let's face it. Understanding other cultures, let alone dealing with them, can be hard work—for both sides (and remember that the room service at least speaks broken English while the hotel guest speaks no Chinese at all). The tongue-in-cheek example above is only the tip of the iceberg. Even when people do you the favor of speaking your language relatively accent-free, you still have to read between the lines, listen for meanings in disguise, and make out where your interlocutor is coming from—in short, be a cross-cultural leader.

Our latest search on Amazon.com for "global leadership" yielded 9,664 books. You'll see that this book is different because it is a synthesis of several powerful methodologies. Twenty-five years ago Insigniam began a journey of catalyzing breakthrough results in the largest companies around the world. Our journey was born of one question: is it possible to take an already successful business and elevate its performance to new, discontinuous levels?

Our proprietary methodology has guided our clients, including 22 percent of the Global 1000, to accomplishments not given by circumstances. In order to see new perspectives and uncover new possibilities, the first step was (and is) to reveal the existing but usually invisible worldview that determines what people think, how they act and interact, and what they see as possible. Another word for this is culture. Every organization is governed by invisible working assumptions and traditional ways of doing business that hinder the identification and pursuit of new growth opportunities. Adopting an "open" mindset is critical for cross-cultural strategy, since innovations and best practices often come not from the headquarters but from the periphery (see Chapter 8 on metanationals).

Did you know that only 7 percent of all communication is verbal while the other 93 percent is nonverbal—facial or body language, hidden in the subtext or the context of the conversation?[2] The potential for misunderstandings is significant and only gets compounded when dealing across cultures and value systems. And companies pay a significant price: to take just one example, a full 40 percent of all expatriates sent to other countries return early because of culture shock. Whenever that happens, the sunk costs of failed assignments include the preview trip (typically with the spouse and the children), the salary, the legal and administrative fees for visa and immigration, the costs of relocation for the employee (again with his or her family), shipping costs for the move, housing costs, schooling costs, taxes and insurance in the target culture; and at the back end, costs of repatriation and reintegration, plus—if things go wrong—the opportunity costs of losing the employee to the competition. If you add it all up, a company stands to lose one million dollars for each expat who fails. And even if expats stay with the company upon their return, most organizations fail to reintegrate them effectively, with unknown costs for missing out on best practices, learning, and strategic intelligence.

But those are peanuts compared to another, much larger cost. Culture clashes have tremendous impact far beyond how you manage your global workforce. They exert a dynamic on strategic collaborations and exacts significant costs when joint ventures go awry. Statistics tell us that more than half of attempted mergers and acquisitions fail, that only one-quarter of large-scale mergers succeed, and that a full 83 percent fail to improve shareholder value.[3] This goes even more for M&A that are cross-border. The failed joint venture of AT&T and Olivetti in the mid-1980s, the ill-conceived merger of BMW with Rover, the famous fiasco of DaimlerChrysler, and the failure of Saab, which General Motors acquired together with Investor AB in 1989, are only the most prominent examples (see Chapter 9 below). The bottom line: culture clash is one of the root causes, and perhaps *the* root cause, of failed M&A. In one survey, 75 percent of companies believed that alliance failure was caused by incompatibility of country or corporate cultures.[4] The costs (both of the sunk and the opportunity kind) can amount to billions of dollars.

This is not to speak of the hidden costs of missed market entry, as Microsoft learned when it lost to Linux in China (see Chapter 1). The global competitive landscape has never been more challenging for a company wanting to achieve growth; turbulence and uncertainty have become the new steady state. In its "Global Risks 2011" survey, the World Economic Forum identified six interconnected risks that were all seen as highly likely and of high impact: fiscal crises, climate change, geopolitical conflict, extreme energy price volatility, economic disparity, and global governance failures. The linchpin connecting all these mega-issues is globalization. This book shows how companies can turn world markets to their advantage. One of the most important books written on managing global leadership in the last ten years, *Culture Clash* provides a methodology for any organization to compete successfully in a new transnational landscape—while minimizing, or better preventing, the unintended but costly consequences of culture clashes.

This book teaches the multicultural skills leaders need to succeed in any culture. It offers both serious and hilarious examples of what can go wrong when we blind ourselves to cultural differences. Through tips, exercises, and lists of do's and don'ts, you and your company can become adept at making things happen across cultures and nations. And by the way, you need not compromise on your goals when you respect local cultures. Virtual leaders take the appropriate cultural pathways while holding fast to their strategic intent.

Proposition: building the global competencies of your enterprise requires a relatively small, high-leverage investment. Leaders who make that investment reap rich benefits in performance while those who fail to invest early on pay an enormous price.

The book comes in ten chapters. Chapter 1 brings together the war stories of our clients and colleagues and distills the ten most costly sins when cultures clash. These situations can be hilarious, but at times dead serious—especially when the costs run into the billions, as the cases of Coca-Cola, DaimlerChrysler, and other multinationals show. Chapter 2 discusses the new global landscape in which leaders must operate and the result of several fundamental changes in the last generation. Chapter 3 explores the impact of language on culture, which allows us to go below the symptom level to the cultural DNA of why people tick a certain way.

Chapter 4 moves on to your own global citizenship and helps you test your cross-cultural IQ. Chapter 5 covers do's and don'ts in dealing with people from any culture, including guidelines written by the legendary Lawrence of Arabia for his fellow British officers in Arab lands, guidelines as relevant now as they were in Sir Lawrence's day. Going beyond best practices,

Chapters 6 and 7 offer systematic tools for avoiding intercultural fiascos and building your enterprise's "global capital."

Chapter 8 shows you a best-practice model: how so-called "metanationals" have turned their company's global savvy into strategic intelligence and innovation assets. Chapter 9 covers cross-border alliances as the acid test of global leadership and gives case studies of successful mergers and acquisitions, for example GE Capital's integration model that the company learned in action by integrating over a hundred acquisitions. Finally, Chapter 10 is about the nuts and bolts of preparing and leading global meetings successfully.

With this methodology, the leaders in our client organizations—which now include 22 percent of Fortune 500 companies—have catalyzed their people to think newly, act differently, and ultimately deliver breakthrough results (over nine billion dollars and counting) across cultures and mindsets—over and over again. We at Insigniam are proud to provide you with the tools you need in your own quest for global leadership.

Preface

Management and national boundaries are no longer congruent.
The scope of management can no longer be politically defined.
National boundaries will continue to be important, but as restraints on
the practice of management, not in defining the practice.[5]
—Peter Drucker

It was a flawless day in September 2001, an Indian-summer morning when the sky was deep blue. I sat on the Brooklyn Promenade—alone except for a few runners and dog walkers. Moments later, at 8:46 am, a plane hit the World Trade Center. Smoke and countless tiny metallic particles were in the air; a light wind swept them toward me. The glitters turned out to be millions of papers flying across the East River. One document I picked up was a page from a civil law book, blackened on all four edges. Another was a FedEx envelope with a contract someone had presumably signed just a few minutes earlier.

About a half-hour later another plane flew in from Staten Island, right over the Statue of Liberty. It flew low and accelerated head-on toward us. It banked like a fighter plane, its dark underbelly visible—a terrifying sight you usually see only in warzones. My reflex was to run for cover. The plane suddenly ducked behind a skyscraper and a moment later disappeared into the South Tower. By this time we were about a dozen people watching, speechless and transfixed. I called as many people as I could on my mobile, but got through only to my parents' answering machine in Sydney before the signal went dead. I saw one tower collapse, then the other. I staggered to a bench, sat down, and wept. It was hard to breathe.

That day of terrible calamity epitomized a clash of cultures, of value systems. And key agencies of the U.S. government were caught off guard by 9/11. Why? Because Americans had lulled themselves into believing that the United States was invulnerable, invincible. They had missed vital intelligence, become lax in their security procedures, and become isolated from much of the world. The material and human costs have been spectacular. In the aftermath of the attacks, the U.S. government was forced to learn a whole new way of gathering intelligence on transnational terrorism. "This is the toughest of all intelligence targets," said Lee Hamilton, the longtime chairman of House committees on intelligence and international relations and a member of the U.S. Commission on National Security. "You have to penetrate their language, their culture."

This is easier said than done. According to the Internet, whose veracity we should of course never question (how's that for Swiss-style sarcasm), here is an actual radio conversation of a U.S. naval ship with Canadian authorities off the coast of Newfoundland. Released by the chief of naval operations, October 10, 1995.[6]

Canadians:	Please divert your course 15 degrees to the south to avoid a collision.
Americans:	Recommend you divert your course 15 degrees to the north to avoid a collision.
Americans:	This is the captain of a U.S. Navy ship. I say again, divert your course.
Canadians:	No, I say again, you divert your course.
Americans:	This is the Aircraft Carrier USS LINCOLN, the second largest ship in the United States Atlantic Fleet. We are accompanied with three Destroyers, three Cruisers, and numerous support vessels. I *demand* that you change your course 15 degrees north. I say again, that's one-five degrees north, or counter-measures will be undertaken to ensure the safety of this ship.

Canadians: This is a lighthouse. Your call.

Whether true or not, stories like these have led to an image of Americans as ignorant bulls in the china shop, which a CNN broadcast in the weeks after the 9/11 terrorist attacks only exacerbated. What was wrong with the picture? It showed Switzerland sandwiched between Germany to the West and Poland to the East (http://www.riehle.org/humorous-takes/fun-photos/ch-according-to-cnn.html). According to CNN, Switzerland had invaded the Czech Republic.

But how can Americans know what is going on in the world if they don't get the information? In the years since the end of the Cold War, U.S. television networks all cut back on foreign bureaus—"a measure of world peace as well as of rich-world insularity," as *The Economist* put it. Network television's world coverage shrank from 45 percent of the news total in the 1970s to 13.5 percent in 1995, a 1997 study by Harvard University found. By 2001 it was down to 6 percent.7 Already in 1998, a study by the University of California at San Diego found that only 2 percent of total newspaper coverage focused on world news, down from 10 percent in 1983. Between 2002 and 2006, the number of foreign-based newspaper correspondents (excluding the *Wall Street Journal,* which publishes Asian and European editions) shrank from 188 to 141. Only 4 U.S. papers—the *Wall Street Journal,* the *Los Angeles Times,* the *New York Times* and the *Washington Post*—still keep a stable of foreign correspondents. *The Baltimore Sun,* which had correspondents from Mexico to Beijing in 1978, now has none. *Newsday,* which once boasted half a dozen foreign bureaus, shut down its last one in 2007 in Pakistan.8

This lack of knowledge has costly, real-world consequences. When American military planes flew over Afghanistan after 9/11 and dropped thousands of packages of food to convince Afghans of the United States' good intentions, it was an unprecedented gesture greeted by many Afghans with enthusiasm. The only problem: the packages, assembled by a food company in Texas, contained such American favorites as peanut butter and jelly and spicy beans and rice, but standard Afghan fare consists mainly of bread, meat, and rice. This endearing story is emblematic for both the twin traits of the American culture: a noble desire to help the world is coupled with ignorance of other cultures.

Against this background of poor and parochial information, U.S. companies must build global competencies—invest in decoding other cultures, gather competitive and human intelligence, and create truly global corporate cultures. Many American managers don't know how to produce results across borders without jeopardizing their missions by stepping on proverbial toes. And let's be clear at the outset: standing in the shoes of the other side is not just nice and morally right. It is strategically smart if you are to fight Al Qaeda and economically indispensable if companies are to compete successfully in the global marketplace.

It's easy to bash Americans, but the truth is that I have yet to see a culture that is without blind spots. (Even the Swiss, who are famed for their integration of diverse languages and cultures, their neutrality, and their mediation capacity, have been known to suffer from cross-cultural blindness.) Hence, while the original edition of *Culture Clash* was geared towards U.S. executives, the revised edition of the book is much more global. Many managers, not just Americans but managers everywhere, assume that the 21st century is yet another American Century. That assumption may come from the past. For example, did you know that by 2010, some 565 million Internet users spoke English, with 510 million Chinese speakers following closely on their heels?[9] With the growth in Internet usage by 301 percent in English-speaking markets compared to 1,479 percent growth in Chinese-speaking markets in the last decade (2000 to 2011), the day is not far off when the #1 language on the Internet will no longer be English but Chinese. The T-Index that shows online market share per country sees Chinese surpassing English by 2015.[10]

Did you know that even in the United States, English is no longer as predominant as it was a generation ago? Now roughly every eighth U.S. resident speaks not English but Spanish, meaning that the United States holds the fifth largest Spanish population, outnumbered only by Mexico, Spain, Argentina, and Colombia. More than every sixth person in New York State is a Spanish speaker; in Texas and California it's 34 percent; and in New Mexico, more than 43 percent—almost every second person. (About 6 percent of Americans speak a mother tongue other than English or Spanish.) The New York Public Library branches in Queens offer books and videos in fifty-nine languages. One Astoria branch carries children's books in Arabic, Bengali, Chinese, Russian, Portuguese, and Gujarati, the official language of the Indian state of Gujarat. And when the library's staff noticed an influx of another immigrant group, they acquired "Ali Baba and the Forty Thieves" in Croatian.[11]

Similarly diverse populations are true for Argentina, Australia, Canada, France, Germany, India, Malaysia, the Netherlands, Singapore, and the United Kingdom, to name but a few. For example, Singapore recognizes four official languages: Malay, English, Mandarin, and Tamil. Indonesia boasts more than 700 different languages. Though predominantly Muslim, it also has large Christian and Hindu populations and its national motto is *Bhinneka tunggal ika* (literally "Many, yet one" or "Unity in Diversity"). And India, the most ethnically diverse nation in the world, counted 122 languages and 234 mother tongues in its 2001 census (which did not even report languages spoken by fewer than 10,000 speakers; that would include 1,652 mother tongues). So even if you never leave your hometown, you are likely to deal with people of vastly different value systems.

More and more top and senior managers at multinationals are not Westerners but stem from the biggest emerging consumer markets; Muhtar Kent, the Turkish-American chairman and CEO of Coca-Cola, and Indra Nooyi, Pepsico's Indian-born chairman and CEO, are just two examples. How many multinationals are prepared for such global diversity? The future growth for many industries, be it pharmaceutical or banking, entertainment or foods, will likely be in these BRICS countries, in all emerging markets. In the age of globalization, companies that ignore these trends and fail to develop their global competencies fall behind and incur huge costs in culture clashes and turf wars, morale slumps and lawsuits, post-merger pains and missed opportunities, or brain drain. The multibillion dollar losses of Coca-Cola in Europe and the DaimlerChrysler failed merger are only the tip of the iceberg.

Speaking of DaimlerChrysler, this ignorance can cut both ways. Executives at several European and Asian clients have told me they don't know how to manage their U.S. subsidiaries effectively, given the vastly different management cultures. The costs on both sides can be enormous. This book aims to teach managers how to minimize such costs and how to build global competencies—a crucial asset in the twenty-first century.

T.D.Z.
Zurich, June 2012

Chapter One

War Stories: The Ten Most Costly Sins When Cultures Collide

Cross-cultural, cross-functional and multilingual knowledge and fluency will be among the most highly valued assets in the emerging managerial landscape, whether one works in a global, regional or national organization.

Mary O'Hara-Devereaux and Robert Johansen, Institute for the Future

George W. Bush:	Condi! Nice to see you. What's happening?
Condoleezza Rice:	Sir, I have the report here about the new leader of China.[12]
Bush:	Great. Lay it on me.
Condi:	Hu is the new leader of China.
Bush:	That's what I want to know.
Condi:	That's what I'm telling you.
Bush:	That's what I'm asking you. Who is the new leader of China?
Condi:	Yes.
Bush:	I mean the fellow's name.
Condi:	Hu.
Bush:	The guy in China.

Condi:	Hu.
Bush:	The new leader of China.
Condi:	Hu.
Bush:	The Chinaman!
Condi:	Hu is leading China.
Bush:	Now whaddya' asking me for?
Condi:	I'm telling you Hu is leading China.
Bush:	Well, I'm asking you. Who is leading China?
Condi:	That's the man's name.
Bush:	That's whose name?
Condi:	Yes.
Bush:	Will you or will you not tell me the name of the new leader of China?
Condi:	Yes, sir.
Bush:	Yassir? Yassir Arafat is in China? I thought he was in the Middle East.
Condi:	That's correct.
Bush:	Then who is in China?
Condi:	Yes, sir.
Bush:	Yassir is in China?
Condi:	No, sir.
Bush:	Then who is?
Condi:	Yes, sir.
Bush:	Yassir?
Condi:	No, sir.

Bush:	Look, Condi. I need to know the name of the new leader of China. Get me the Secretary General of the U.N. on the phone.
Condi:	Kofi?
Bush:	No, thanks.
Condi:	You want Kofi?
Bush:	No.
Condi:	You don't want Kofi.
Bush:	No. But now that you mention it, I could use a glass of milk. And then get me the U.N.
Condi:	Yes, sir.
Bush:	Not Yassir! The guy at the U.N.
Condi:	Kofi?
Bush:	Milk! Will you please make the call?
Condi:	And call who?
Bush:	Who is the guy at the U.N?
Condi:	Hu is the guy in China.
Bush:	Will you stay out of China?!
Condi:	Yes, sir.
Bush:	And stay out of the Middle East! Just get me the guy at the U.N.
Condi:	Kofi.
Bush:	All right! With cream and two sugars. Now get on the phone.

(Condi picks up the phone.)

Condi:	Rice, here.
Bush:	Rice? Good idea. And a couple of egg rolls, too. Maybe we should send some to the guy in China. And the Middle East. Can you get Chinese food in the Middle East?

Miscommunications like the fake one above happen all the time, and as the example shows, they even happen between members of the same tribe. In fact, they might happen more easily when people speak the same language and assume they know what the other person is saying. Take the Austrian army of the nineteenth century, where officers showed their familiarity by addressing each other with the familiar *Du* form of "you" used elsewhere only for friends or servants, rather than the more formal *Sie* normally used in German-speaking society. In World War I, when Austria allied itself with Emperor Wilhelm II's Germany, German officers felt themselves being insulted or, worse, propositioned by their Austrian colleagues who addressed them with the intimate *Du.*

Such cultural misunderstandings continue to this day. Most of us know this story: Chevrolet introduced its Chevy Nova model in the Latin American market, but was puzzled to find virtually no demand. Too late, the company found out that "Nova" was understood as *no va,* "does not work."

Far fewer people have heard the more recent tales of hilarious marketing mistakes when cultures collide.[13]

- The U.S. Dairy Board ran into problems when it tried to translate its widely promoted Got Milk campaign for the Hispanic market. "Got Milk" in Spanish came out as *Tienes Leche?* which means: "Are you Lactating?"
- Coors put its slogan, "Turn it loose," into Spanish, where it was read as something like "Suffer from diarrhea."
- Clairol introduced the "Mist Stick," a curling iron, in

Germany only to find out that *"Mist"* is German slang for manure (or worse, a four-letter word). Few customers had use for the "manure stick."

- The American slogan for Salem cigarettes, "Salem—Feeling Free," was translated for the Japanese market as "When smoking Salem, you will feel so refreshed that your mind seems to be free and empty."

- When Gerber started selling baby food in Africa, it used the same packaging as in the United States, with the baby on the label. Only later did the Swiss company learn that since most people in Africa don't read English, companies routinely put pictures on the label of what is inside the container.

- Colgate introduced a toothpaste in France called Cue, the name of a notorious pornographic magazine.

- An American T-shirt maker in Miami printed shirts for the Spanish market to promote the Pope's visit. The company made one tiny mistake—instead of "I saw the Pope" *(el Papa),* the shirts read "I saw the potato" *(la papa).*

- In Italy, a campaign for Schweppes Tonic Water translated the name into "Schweppes Toilet Water."

- Pepsi's "Come alive with the Pepsi Generation" translated into Chinese came out as "Pepsi brings your ancestors back from the grave."

- Frank Perdue's chicken slogan "it takes a strong man to make a tender chicken" was translated into Spanish as "it takes an aroused man to make a chicken affectionate."

- When Parker Pen marketed a ballpoint pen in Mexico, its ads were supposed to read, "It won't leak in your pocket and embarrass you." Instead, the company thought that the word *embarazar* (to impregnate) meant to embarrass, so the ad read: "It won't leak in your pocket and make you pregnant."

- And my favorite: the Scandinavian vacuum manufacturer Electrolux used as its slogan in an American campaign: "Nothing sucks like an Electrolux."

These examples are marketing faux-pas. What about other missteps, in leadership, management, operations, or even daily living? The airline industry abounds in amusing misunderstandings. Take this exchange from 2006 between an Air China pilot and an air traffic controller at New York's Kennedy airport (ATC is the air traffic controller, 981 is the Air China pilot. For the full culture clash and the increasingly exasperated voice of the controller, check out the YouTube video):

ATC: Air China 981, make the right turn here at Juliette, join Alpha, hold short of MikeAlpha.

981: Right on Juliette, hold shit . . . uhh . . . Taxi Alpha, hold November. (. . .) Can we taxi now?

ATC: Make the right turn at Juliette, join Alpha, hold short of MikeAlpha—Air China 981.

981: Air China 981, roger, join right Juliette, join Alpha, hold short to November.

ATC: OK I will say it again, hold short of MikeAlpha, "M-A," MIKEALPHA, NOT November.

981: OK, hold short of MikeAlpha, 981.

ATC: Air China 981, have they cleared you into the ramp?

981: Roger, ramp to the . . . ramp, Air China 981.

ATC: OK, they have cleared you into the ramp?

ATC: Air China 981, ground? . . .

ATC: Air China 981, Kennedy ground?

981: 981, go ahead.

ATC: Have you been cleared into the ramp?

981: OK, cleared to the ramp?

ATC: No, that was a question! Have the ramp people cleared you into the gate?

981: Roger to the gate, Air China 981.

ATC: I'll try it again, it's a question, hold your position, this is a question, (. . .) an interrogative, HAVE YOU BEEN CLEARED INTO YOUR GATE?

981: OK, we hold here.

ATC: OK, how about the question, have they cleared you into the gate?

981: (. . .) Tower (. . .) Ground, Air China 981, we are uhh, Gate number 3 is open, we are taxi to the northern.

ATC: Air China 981, taxi to the ramp.

981: Roger, taxi ramp.[14]

Unfortunately, language barriers in air traffic can be much less amusing. The list of deadly accidents when things got lost in translation is long. Just one example: in 1977, two Boeing 747s collided on a runway at Tenerife in the Canary Islands. The disaster in which 583 people died happened in a dense fog, but contributing factors were misunderstandings of orders and acknowledgments between the aircraft on the runway and the air traffic controllers.[15]

Your War Stories?

When you work in or with another culture, it's often the small stuff that can throw a wrench into the well-oiled machinery of your routines (see the photo on the next page) and in those moments, despite the well-known adage, you really do sweat the small stuff.

One executive told me she was on a business trip to France when her computer crashed, forcing her to use the Apple Macbook Pro of one of her French colleagues. She was in for a surprise: Several keys on the keyboard were either where she least expected them (where the Y should have been, there now

(Source: AFP/Getty Images)

was the Z, and vice versa; when she typed a colon, she got an é; and the @ sign was nowhere near the Shift-2 function). She was lucky if the keyboard showed symbols at all (where had the # sign gone?). Dealing with these changes was a minor inconvenience, but it cost her time and turmoil. (Similarly, two American managers on a business trip to Paris wanted to take an unexpected day to walk around the city, and decided to buy sneakers for easy walking. The sneakers were hard to come by, as French people generally do not use sneakers for walking, only for sports or fashion.) So it's not just the big culture clashes, but it can also be the details of everyday life that can trip you up or, at least, wear you down.

In one business meeting in Southeast Asia, one of my colleagues sat down and crossed her legs once the session had begun. She noticed a moment later that the room had turned eerily quiet and that several participants looked at her askance. It was strange, and she had the distinct feeling that she had done something inappropriate, but no idea what—until one of the local leaders took her aside on the break and told her she had committed an unpardonable sin: She had shown the soles of her feet, which is a sign of disrespect in Asian cultures, tantamount to sticking up your middle finger in the West.

A U.S. executive once told us that one of his direct reports, a Mexican, was a "shifty guy." Much later it became clear that the co-worker had been trained by his culture to be deferent to leaders by never looking his boss in the eye and never addressing him directly. The U.S. boss had completely misread his behavior as "dishonest."

Examples of misunderstanding that undermine business performance are far too many. In the early 1990s Insigniam was called into a manufacturing facility in Puerto Rico that belonged to a multinational pharmaceutical company. The consulting intervention came about as a result of a consent decree by the FDA, the first in the industry and unheard of in Puerto Rico in those days. Insigniam's mandate was to accelerate the manufacturing recertification process without burning out the workers. Working at a pharma company in Puerto Rico meant very high status, and the factory workers prided themselves in working there; and pride matters in all cultures and perhaps nowhere more so than in the Latin cultures. The problem was that being under regulatory action made the workers feel ashamed with their families and neighbors for working with this company. They called the client dismissively "this North American company." What made it worse is that the Puerto Ricans saw the swarms of "North American" executives dispatched to execute the corrective action plans as condescending and lording it (i.e. their compliance problems) over them, which in their eyes added insult to injury on a daily basis. Not to be outdone, the North Americans complained of the huge ego needs and sensitivity of the manufacturing leaders and work force. The result: not only was the momentum needed for success lacking, the turnaround was jeopardized too.

On another occasion Insigniam co-founder Shideh Bina

facilitated a strategy design session with a group of Latin executives that consisted entirely of men from Argentina, Brazil, Mexico, and Spain. They were satisfied with Shideh's facilitation and the desired work outputs, but expressed some dissatisfaction that she had left out some topics from the agenda (despite asking her to take almost three hours out of the session to watch Argentina compete in the World Cup). When she corrected for that in the next session and drove the meeting to cover everything on the agenda, they politely slowed their cooperation and grumbled about her not understanding the ways of their regions, inferring she was a controlling and dominating American. While Shideh finally restored the goodwill with several mea culpas, combined with a good dinner bonding session when she joined the men in eating grilled worms, cooked ants and fungi grown on corn husks, the incident illustrates the cultural landmines that often must be navigated.

Moving to Asia, one U.S. executive worked on an assignment in China with a large U.S.-based multinational that had just acquired a B2B business from a Chinese entrepreneur for tens of millions of dollars. The executive knew of course that this being China, people didn't vote, they did not live in a democracy, they were part of a socialist planned economy. Yet now the entrepreneur and each member of his five-person executive team had become capitalists and millionaires. What was astonishing was how much the cultural background context of state-run planning shaped the executives' leadership and relationships. Throughout the meeting, this culture led to a conspiracy of silence: they spoke amongst themselves instead of saying what they thought. It would take six months of continuous effort to shift that behavior.

Even in Turkey, with all its aspirations to be a bridge between Europe and Asia, business people may not necessarily embrace open discussions of politics. My French colleague, Guillaume Pajeot, was on assignment in Istanbul and found himself in a discussion over lunch with some participants in a leadership program about the integration of Kurds in modern

Turkey. "Big mistake," Guillaume recalled. "The cultural clash was: I expected a certain openness about discussing this kind of topics with this type of executive from a global company (well educated, diverse, Westernized Turks) just as I experience them in Europe. This was completely inappropriate and I got a complaint offline from a director."

Guillaume co-led a breakthrough work session at a leading pharma company in 2008 with clinical research assistants from Central and Eastern European countries, from Estonia to Bosnia, Czech Republic to Russia. The intent of the sessions was to accelerate cycle time on a new drug being developed. Their boss attended the work session to learn new competencies. "No one in the room would interact with us about the issues they were facing in their development program. Speaking up and openly discussing issues in a group was completely foreign in their culture." Repeatedly prodded by Guillaume, the participants finally acknowledged that their reluctance to speak up stemmed from their education in former communist countries where speaking up had put their lives at risk. "Even when the boss said it was okay to speak up and that she would not chop their heads off, they did not participate more." They simply did not trust the boss's intentions. Guillaume realized that creating the conditions for breakthrough work in Eastern European cultures requires pre-work, interviews, and prior alignment on clear rules about what can and what cannot be discussed. "We missed this cultural difference with what we had experienced so far in other parts of the world."

Back in the West, the exact same behavior can have totally different meanings in two different cultures, as we saw in the example of the "shifty" Mexican manager above. When I worked late, in the U.S. business culture that was typically seen as a sign of my commitment and dedication to the job. In Switzerland or Germany, working late meant almost the opposite: that I was not on top of things and that I had to stay late because I failed to effectively delegate my accountabilities.

Another transatlantic culture clash: one senior manager had long been trained as a salesperson to find personal things to connect and get prospective clients to talk. Asking questions about people's lives had become her standard procedure for building and cultivating work relationships. But when she did business in France, she was seen as prying inappropriately in the private sphere of her European clients. Several client executives advised her to stop violating people's privacy boundaries. To top it off, one German executive asked her, "Are you always so nosy?"

You don't even have to cross the Atlantic to experience culture clashes: crossing the U.S. border to Canada can be enough. After moving to Canada, my colleague Ashley Tappan "assumed, because they were an English speaking country and a North American country, we would have the same views—we did not. Also, being from the United States, I began my life 'abroad' proudly proclaiming my American status. When I learned that it was considered at best 'so what?' and at worst overbearing and arrogant, I stopped leading with my nationality or even with *me*. I got focused on being interested in *them*."

At another pharma company, some of my colleagues were dealing with a doctor who was Swedish. "We complemented her on more than one occasion for her consistent and immense contribution to the project—she was an excellent example of an informal leader. What we did not know was that in the Swedish culture, there is a way of being and even a word, *lagom*." The Swedish–English dictionary defines lagom as 'enough, sufficient, adequate, just right' and that is often translated as 'in moderation.'" The notion of *lagom* is a core value in the Swedish culture: "stay in the middle," don't be extreme, don't do anything that draws the spotlight to you, and don't single people out. Of course this cultural preference has implications for—or in this case against—leadership. The executive was very uncomfortable with being singled out by the public appreciation heaped on her, and my colleagues realized only later that, while their intentions had been right, "we had taken the wrong approach."

The Ten Most Costly Sins When Cultures Clash

We have seen that cross-cultural misunderstandings can be hilarious, but they all too often lead to strategic failures and billion-dollar fiascos, which is no laughing matter. Motorola's flameout was one of the more spectacular. The company deployed its Iridium global satellite system to offer truly global telephone service, but its global strategy was out of touch with the global realities. When Iridium was shut down, its sunk cost to Motorola was $3.5 billion. Iridium is just one of countless examples. Here are the ten most costly sins you and your company should avoid when doing business in other cultures.

Sin #1: You think the world plays by your rules

We have already seen that few places anywhere are unaffected by Americanization. Almost anywhere in the world people can buy from Amazon, listen to Bruce Springsteen or Snow Patrol, get coveted Abercrombie & Fitch T-shirts or Victoria's Secret panties or Apple iPads or Hollywood DVDs (as our older daughter does, and believe me, our younger daughter learned "iPhone" and "Nemo" as fixtures in her vocabulary before she learned "Thank you"). Americans eat hamburgers or bagels (pronounced "begols") in Paris or at Dunkin' Donuts in Rome—if they even leave the United States. Reportedly less than 15 percent of U.S. managers own a passport. For many Americans, the United States is evidently the whole world.

In the 1990s the U.S. management model of unfettered capitalism—free markets, free agents, deregulation, low taxes, individual accountability, management by objectives—were hailed as the underpinnings of economic growth anywhere in the world. The European and Japanese model of the welfare state and social responsibility seemed a relict of the past. But now, according to the Global Competitiveness Report published annually by the World Economic Forum,[16] the most competitive nation worldwide is no longer the United States but Switzerland, which many would consider a welfare state. Since

2000, the United States has dropped from rank two to five, after Singapore, Sweden, and Finland. Seven of the top ten are European countries. American managers might learn something from Europeans, for example the ability to manage diversity and multiculturalism in a multilingual European Union.

In Chapter 8, you will read below about Pepsi's travails with utilizing precious water resources in India; Coca-Cola has had its share of issues in Europe, which has at times been a desert without refreshment in sight. The company learned the hard way that the rest of the world is not simply an extension of the United States. Already in 1999 the Italian Antitrust Authority had fined Coke more than $16 million for keeping competitors out through illegal discounts, bonuses, and exclusive deals with wholesalers and retailers, since in Europe the threshold for "dominant position" can be as low as 40 percent, while under the U.S. Sherman Antitrust Act, monopoly power requires well over 50 percent market share. The company also found itself under scrutiny for taking undue advantage of its near-monopoly when European regulators scaled back Coke's acquisition of Cadbury Schweppes' non-U.S. beverage business from $1.85 billion to $1.1 billion. Worse, the same year, French courts rebuffed its coveted purchase of the best-known French soda brand Orangina. To add insult to injury, a year later Cadbury Schweppes bought Orangina.

Sin #2: You do what you always did in the past

A bigger blow came in June 1999 when some thirty Belgian school children got sick with nausea, abdominal pains, vomiting, and diarrhea from drinking soda from a contaminated Coca-Cola shipment.[17] The company did what it had always done: it insisted—with characteristic American optimism—that the problem was minor and not a health hazard, and failed to properly warn the European public of the dangers. For several weeks the company did not fully acknowledge, explain, or apologize for this outbreak. The problem escalated until at least two hundred more people became ill in Belgium and France. Several governments ordered Coke off the shelves. These calamities and damage to Coca-Cola's reputation could have easily been prevented by creating a truly global corporate culture and by building some basic cross-cultural skills for top managers at the company's Atlanta headquarters. The very thing that had always been its success formula now cost the beverage giant multibillion dollar losses in sales, a huge setback in public relations, and a plunge in shareholder value.

Coca-Cola learned its lesson. In 2001 it collaborated with the French government and voluntarily recalled shipments that were possibly contaminated. More importantly, Coke now aspires to respect diversity and local leaders. "You can't apply a global standard of measurement to consumers," Coke's former chairman and CEO Douglas Daft once told me, "because it reduces everything to the lowest common denominator." Daft knew about cross-cultural skills. An Australian, he had risen through the ranks for thirty years and had long been based in Asia. Virtually a stranger in Atlanta headquarters when he succeeded Douglas Ivester, Daft swiftly decentralized decision-making to the local level and embraced local brands and flavors. (Coke is not out of the woods yet: its European sales fell 3 percent in the first quarter of 2011.)

Sin #3: You take English for granted

True, English is the Number One world language and is even encroaching on the turf of other languages. In Germany, English is the most widely studied foreign language in schools, and a mixed language called "Denglisch" is becoming more and more fashionable. Audi promises you "die (the in German) power." Lufthansa's slogan is, "Thinking in new directions." Volkswagen launched the "New Beetle." "New Beetle sounds more hip than neuer *Käfer*," said Sabina Metzner of Volkswagen. "We wanted to make clear that the Beetle might have some resemblances to the old *Käfer*, but it is very much a modern car."

Not everybody is thrilled. A professor of economics at the University of Dortmund was so disgusted with the "spineless conformity" of Denglisch that he founded the Society for the Protection of the German Language (now Verein Deutsche Sprache, Association German Language) and instituted an annual booby prize for the "Sprachpanscher" ("language diluter") of the year.[18] Membership has soared to 34,000.

But isn't it simpler if we all speak the same language world-wide? "Natürlich können sich Manager auf Englisch verständigen" (oops, that was German, sorry!) "Of course managers can communicate in English," said Porsche's former chairman Wendelin Wiedeking. "But that is not the case on all work levels. It gets quite difficult when it's about details, for example engine parts. But precisely in these matters, workers must understand each other perfectly."[19]

And language is not just about communication. As the German philosopher Martin Heidegger wrote, language is the house of being: it reflects cultural essence. Sony's founder Akio Morita, who became one of the best-loved Japanese people in the West during the twentieth century, once gave a great example in a TV interview, saying that when Westerners "ask questions or express an opinion, they want to know right away whether the other party agrees or opposes them. So in English, 'yes' or 'no' comes first. We Japanese prefer to save the 'yes' or 'no' for last. Particularly when the answer is 'no,' we put off saying that as long as possible, and they find that exasperating." Morita created a private club for business leaders whose motto was inscribed above the bar: "We Japanese businessmen must be amphibians. We must survive in water and on land," in the incompatible worlds of East and West.[20]

Sin #4: You don't respect the cultural pathways for making things happen

Coke is not alone; other U.S. multinationals have been on the defensive in Europe because of simple faux pas in their cross-cultural business dealings. When Disney built its EuroDisney theme park in Paris, it triggered a visceral hate campaign among the Paris intelligentsia, and angry French people boycotted EuroDisney en masse. The company had tailored the theme park on its U.S. parks model. Practices that had made sense in the United States enraged the French: EuroDisney's kiosks failed to serve the wine and local food that many French people love. Disney's screening process for job applicants was an affront to accepted socialist beliefs in France. The company's calamities inspired ridicule. A trendy French magazine delighted in comparing the long-term impact of EuroDisney to that of a nuclear bomb and listed the radioactive fallout at point zero, at ten miles from point zero, at fifty miles, and so forth. It took Disney years and a new (French) company president to make basic adjustments, restore its image, and meet EuroDisney's profitability goals. Small wonder that fist-swinging farmers like José Bové achieved the status of résistance heroes by vandalizing McDonald's facilities in France—admirers call Bové their "Robin Hood."

Like Coke, other companies have stepped on regulatory toes. In late 2000, a French court ordered Yahoo to bar French citizens from Nazi items on its web site. From a French legal perspective, the case was clear: Yahoo was breaking the law. In the United States, the case was equally clear: the French ruling amounted to censorship and violated the First Amendment. Both perspectives were right, depending on where you stood. It goes to show how profoundly culture and customs shape the reality we see.

Sin #5: You don't stand in your host's shoes

Another technology company, Microsoft, came to suffer in France too. To top off the French battle against Americanization, one report commissioned by the French defense ministry accused Microsoft of using its systems to spy for the CIA. But while the giant from Redmond could shrug off the allegation by

France, China dealt it a more serious blow. To launch Windows 95 in China, Microsoft had the operating system translated into Chinese. The company made one tiny cross-cultural mistake: failing to stand in the shoes of its Chinese customer, it used programmers in Taiwan to write the software. Chinese government officials who looked at the operating system were in for a bad surprise: the software was programmed to display references to "communist bandits" and to exhort users to "take back the mainland." Furious with Microsoft, the Chinese government decided to back Linux instead—a decision disastrous for Microsoft in a country that is now the second-largest hardware market in the world.

Microsoft learned from its early mistakes. In 1999, Bill Gates sent Craig Mundie, who then headed the company's public policy efforts and later became its chief research and strategy officer, to figure out why Microsoft was so reviled in China. On the trip Mundie had an epiphany. "I remember going back to Redmond and saying, 'Our business is just broken in China.'" Mundie concluded that the company was assigning executives too junior and that selling activities were overemphasized. "But where we were most broken," he said, "was that our business practices and our engagement did not reflect the importance of having a collaborative approach with the government."

Mundie started visiting China four or five times a year. He brought twenty-five of the company's one hundred vice presidents for a week-long "China Immersion Tour." He hired former Secretary of State Henry Kissinger to advise him and open doors.

And he told leaders that Microsoft wanted to help China develop its own software industry, an urgent government priority. The company even commissioned a McKinsey study for Chinese officials in 2001 that, among other things, recommended improving the protection of intellectual property.[21]

By 2007, the company had turned around its fortunes through a set of key initiatives: inviting China to participate in a program to view the Windows source code and even make modifications, an unprecedented step; opening a major research center in Beijing; building strong relationships with the Chinese government; and offering a precipitous price drop to seven to ten dollars per seat. The interventions paid off: Windows and Office became the undisputed software leader in China, and Gates an honorary trustee of Peking University. Each intervention was founded on one principle: collaboration and standing in the shoes of the other side.

The same cannot be said of one of the top U.S. investment banks, which were launching new policies in Europe and forgot to ask the Europeans what they thought about these policies. The Europeans didn't like not being consulted. They would have liked having a voice in the outcome. After our intervention, the U.S. middle managers started listening, the kickoff conference became a success, and the Europeans embraced the new picture. But before that, the bank's people in New York were wondering why most Europeans did not return their calls. The Europeans basically stopped interacting with global headquarters, since in their experience headquarters was unable or unwilling—or both—to see the world from their point of view.

Sin #6: You forget to invest in relationships

Executives at another New York-based Fortune 500 investment bank complained bitterly that their European counterparts completely ignored their communications. After some prodding I found that the Americans had never even bothered to create partnerships with the Europeans. They would call London or Frankfurt on Friday morning Eastern Time, just before the weekend Greenwich Mean Time, and tell people, "Can you just send me this report by the end of business today?" Their requests for action had no foundation in relationship. Not a good idea.

It is easy to talk about other people's mistakes, but I made plenty of my own. I learned about the value of relationship-building the hard and painful way in 1987 during a four-month assignment in India. The CEO of the organization I was to work with was out of town when I arrived (come to think of it, her absence was a tell-tale sign), and had sent her deputy to meet me at the airport. In my youthful impatience, rather than wait for the CEO to return, I decided to meet with the deputy and launch into work immediately. It was the biggest mistake I could have made. Not only did I fail to create the relationship and trust necessary to conduct business effectively, but I also imposed my will on my host country. The CEO, feeling that I had bypassed her authority, mistrusted me from the start and attempted to undermine my efforts. She, and many of my Indian colleagues, saw me as an intruder who was meddling with their operation. I ultimately got the job done, but my impatience and insensitivity had thrown an unnecessary wrench into my own project.

I later learned from a colleague of mine who had been on a similar assignment that he had been much smarter. When he arrived in India, there were no meetings, no reception, not one phone call from the people with whom he had come to work. This went on for a week or so. He kept himself busy reading, settling in to his apartment, and learning about the culture. The next week the head of the organization called him and asked, "What do you want?" He said, "Let's meet and see what *you* want." He was ready to work, and made clear that he had come to be of service, rather than imposing himself and his agenda in Western fashion as I did. His work had been successful, and graceful.

Another factor would also have made a difference in my trip: more conscious preparation and alignment beforehand. My trip had been set up on a short and perfunctory conference call. A senior executive at global headquarters announced to the CEO in India that I would come there to work. Confronted with that news, the CEO said the polite thing you are expected to say in India: "Great!" I discovered later that she had never endorsed the trip. What I should have done before going was to call and find out what she wanted, and to build or verify a demand for my services. My visit was jeopardized before I got on the plane.

In 1990, when I was based indefinitely in Japan (but ended up staying only seven months), I made sure not to make the same mistake again. I verified through several conference calls with the CEO in Tokyo that he indeed had a high demand for my coaching, and I kept a low profile until I had built a sufficient base of relationship. A fun side effect: I drank a lot of sake with my Japanese colleagues and investors—the socializing glue of drinking is virtually the only accepted avenue for Japanese executives to get acquainted with each other. Like Coke's Daft, I came to appreciate the value of relationships and "face time."

But in actuality, this didn't go all that smoothly either. After I arrived, the management of the host organization gave me a gorgeous apartment in a Tokyo high-rise with an incredible view, a table shaped like a baby grand piano, a great video and sound system. I felt like a king. After about two-and-a-half weeks, I was told quietly but in no uncertain terms that I'd "better move out." I said, "No problem. When?" "Today." "Today?" My grace period had come to an abrupt end. I had nowhere to go. I ended up finding a tiny apartment in the printing district of Kasuga. Had I done anything to deserve such brusque treatment? I will never know. That is part of the mystery of living in Japan. You never know if you just made a mistake or even committed a capital sin, because you may not find out for ten years, if ever.

It took me months to recreate the relationship and reestablish my credibility (assuming I had ever had it). I listened a lot. I was in many meetings where I stayed silent and attentive, seeking to be part of the consensus. I felt like a low-level samurai warrior, condemned to doing only what I was told to do, nothing more and nothing less. Then, one day in the fall, something shifted. The CEO invited me to accompany him to the bathhouse. That was how he conveyed to me that he was ready to take our relationship to the next level. I felt like I was being knighted. I was elated—until I stepped up to the hot tub, that is. The water was so hot that I could almost not bear getting in; the CEO barely suppressed a chuckle as I got into the steamy water.

Afterwards, he and I lay on massage tables as stocky, sixty-year-old women performed a kind of dance on our backs. The women pointed at my body hair and giggled; I figured they had probably never worked on a Westerner before. I must have seemed quite like a monkey to them.

But the bottom line was that the CEO had graced me with his invitation. From then on, I was his partner (no small feat, given that even today some Japanese university libraries still carry books that "prove" the inferiority of the Western brain compared to the Japanese brain). Although it had seemed terribly inefficient to a Westerner, my careful relationship building paid off in the end. He and I produced extraordinary financial results together. (He even suggested at one point that I should marry a Japanese woman and settle there, a suggestion which, in true Japanese style, I never declined openly.)

Unpleasant surprises are the rule in unfamiliar cultural settings. I will never forget the lunches I had with my friend Mikio Uekusa, the owner and president of Akebono Inc. and a key investor, at his company headquarters—particularly the first one. Uekusa-san's personal secretary brought us each a black, lacquered box containing our lunch. The box was beautiful, but the contents were not. I peaked inside and shivered at the sight of the jello-like, milky, translucent substance. Forcing a broad smile on my face, I used the elegant wooden chopsticks to take a piece of one of the blubbery masses. It tasted awful. My smile disappeared, but I tried to put it back on. What to do? If I wanted Uekusa-san to place the calls I had asked him to make to other $100,000 investors, I knew I had to enjoy the food that he so generously provided. While I discreetly looked for a plant to spit the food into—but found none—I tasted the white substance, almost choked on it, and lied that it was "delicious." (Reminiscing about these lunches much later, I came to think that Uekusa-san must have been testing me, and probably laughed his head off behind my back.) After lunch, I pulled out my investor list, dialed the phone, and handed the receiver to

Uekusa-san, all with nauseous vengeance. Virtually every call produced a $100,000 investor.

I learned two lessons from this experience. The first is obvious: when in Rome, do as the Romans do. Second, and more importantly, I saw how important it is to keep hold of your objective while taking the appropriate cultural pathways to achieve that intent. You must be committed to your strategic intent, yet you must also be flexible about doing whatever the particular culture demands. It may not be a straight shot. It may feel as though you are wasting time, particularly if you are a Westerner, because you will not be doing what you would in your own culture. The inverse is just as true: if you stem from the East, you might feel, for example, that Western collaborators are overly focused on their individualism, or that they move into the business at hand much too quickly. My work in Japan required a deep investment in relationship and socializing, doing strange things and going to unfamiliar places. Coupled with a steadfast commitment to the end goal, the investment paid off.

Sin #7: You jump from vision to action

But I had no time to rest on my laurels. The year's end was fast approaching, and neither the Europeans nor the Americans came through on their funding commitments to global headquarters. On one of our global executive team calls, the chief operating officer at the time decided to override my objections and come to Tokyo with his three most trusted lieutenants to bail the global office out. They arrived sometime in December, which left a ridiculously short timeline before Christmas and the New Year to fill a multimillion dollar hole in the global funding budget. The Japanese CEO said diplomatically that he did not really see the usefulness of such an intervention, but that he trusted the global office leadership.

We tried to mobilize the Tokyo staff to produce a financial miracle. The attempt failed miserably, and the fundamental trust of our Japanese partners for the global office was shattered. To this day I do not know whether the Japanese have forgiven the

global headquarters for going in without creating a shared strategy. For years and years afterwards, even though I was director
of global operations, the Japanese subsidiary refused my
requests or feigned not to understand them. Our relationship
was cordial on the surface, but had become testy and reserved
underneath. If I brought up the subject of money head-on, I
might lose the entire relationship; if I tip-toed around the issue,
I had no money. So I ended up with a little of both.

The lesson: unlike in Japan, in the United States Nike's
credo "Just Do It" reigns supreme. "Just Do It" in this case
translated into "Let's just go to Japan," implying that once we
were on the ground, we would somehow find our way through.
Learning by doing is one of the tenets that made the United
States a great haven for entrepreneurship and innovation, but
over-reliance on learning by doing can backfire in a culture that
emphasizes the process and the How. Managers must put in the
other building blocks of accomplishment—relationship, vision,
strategy—before taking action. This is true not only for Japan: in
Central and Northern Europe, for example, the How—the bridge
between vision and action—must be crystal clear to people,
preferably in writing, before they take action. So if you go into a
meeting in Germany or Sweden, be sure to brief the participants
on your plans, your proposal, or your agenda beforehand so as
to minimize surprises and crisis management.

Sin #8: You take the village by storm

Unfortunately American companies seldom recognize this problem. A colleague told me that when General Electric launched a
new initiative in Hungary, the Americans in charge got off the
plane, did a dog-and-pony show of the GE core values, and left.
One "victim" of this "storming of the village" told her that this
was the "exact same thing the Russians did—just no tanks."

Another example: one American investment banker sought
to buy a private bank in Switzerland. When he arrived for a first
exploratory meeting with the bank's owners in the small town

where they lived, he opened the meeting by saying that his train would leave very soon, pulled out the draft contract, and asked if they could get right down to business. The owners just smiled politely and said good-bye. Of course it never came to a second meeting, let alone a transaction. The investment banker's pushy attitude had been a deal-breaker.

Let me, however, balance out the impression that U.S. multinationals are the only culprits. It takes two to tango, and many a cross-cultural gaffe originates in Europe. Without the least bit of *Schadenfreude* (an untranslatable German word for glee at the misfortune of others), I recall my prediction in a speech in mid-1999 that the merger of Mercedes and Chrysler would fall on its face. The writing was on the wall: just ten months after the merger that created DaimlerChrysler, the American top executive in charge of integrating the operations in Stuttgart with those in Auburn Hills resigned. Though touting DaimlerChrysler as a "merger of equals," Europeans dominated the new entity from the start. Co-chairman Jürgen Schrempp put himself firmly in charge, pushed all but two Americans from the management board of the combined company, and installed his trusted German aide Dieter Zetsche at Chrysler's helm.

DaimlerChrysler paid dearly for this new brand of German imperialism: by 2001, the company's revenue had fallen by 13 percent, operating profits by 75 percent, forcing it to eliminate 26,000 jobs and suffer major brain drain from the loss of some of Chrysler's most creative talent. Although Zetsche succeeded Schrempp as CEO of the combined company in 2005 and proved to be a much more diplomatic leader, DaimlerChrysler never quite recovered from its early mistakes. In March 2007 it reported a 7.7 percent loss in sales, and Chrysler was forced to lay off another 13,000 people. Two months later Daimler divorced Chrysler, selling it off to Cerberus Capital Management and ending what had once been touted as a "marriage made in heaven." (Chrysler was subsequently bailed out by the U.S. government, and Fiat purchased a majority stake in the company.)

Carlos Ghosn, who was born in Brazil, grew up in Lebanon, and is a citizen of France, might serve as a great counter-example to Schrempp. In 1999 he was sent to Japan by Renault when the French company had bought 36.8 percent of Nissan. His mission: to restructure and revive the ailing Japanese car manufacturer. His promise: to post a profit for the fiscal year ending March 2001. His process: closing factories, axing thousands of jobs, and cutting off small, money-losing affiliates. These radical changes would have hardly endeared Ghosn to the Japanese, who were known to push back against foreign managers. But the improbable happened: Ghosn succeeded, his autobiography sold 150,000 in the first month, and he became a comic book star—probably the highest honor in comic-crazed Japan. Today he is the chief of Renault. What was Ghosn's main recipe for success? He recognized the power of building trust and involving your global partners in your vision and strategy. One of his moves that secured him credibility was his pledge that if Nissan did not turn around, he would be the first to go. But the bottom line was that he was willing to listen to all key stakeholders before making tough decisions.

Sin #9: You select the wrong people

Then again, managers may have put the right people in the wrong expatriate jobs to begin with. All too often, senior managers move executives to a target country based on their technical or financial or operational skills alone, rather than also on their cross-cultural expertise; or they get the mix of expats and local leaders wrong. "We don't do a very good job of selecting people for foreign postings," concedes Sir Brian Pitman, chairman of Lloyds Group PLC. The British bank sent a brilliant young executive to Argentina. "He only lasted one week," Pitman said. "He just didn't fit in." The problem is, people will decide very quickly and reflexively whether or not to accept you. Comedian Jerry Seinfeld said once that the challenge of being funny never lets up: no matter how funny you were five minutes ago, the audience is unforgiving. Five minutes of bad jokes, and you have lost them.[22]

Sin #10: You forget that your advice is noise in their ears

The final high-cost mistake you can make is to fail building a demand for your actions. When I was based in India, it took me months to realize that I was dispensing unsolicited advice. And when there is no demand for it, even your best advice turns into noise pollution. A few weeks into my assignment, it dawned on me that telling people what to do made no difference; what was needed was not giving answers but asking questions and listening.

Most people in most places have a good reason, at least subjectively, for doing what they do. Barging in and imposing changes is of course always possible, but should be only a last resort. Your change efforts will meet with resistance unless you can create a demand for your intervention and end up with people as owners of the changes they need to make. Even in the change-happy United States, where many see change as an adventure, resistance can be high. So how would you react if an executive from Switzerland or Japan came in and told you how to run things—which is reportedly how things work at the U.S. subsidiary of a major Japanese automaker in Chicago, where every U.S. executive has a Japanese shadow partner who doesn't let them out of sight, monitors their every move, and has veto power over their every decision?

And if expats fit in beautifully with their host culture, a common mistake multinationals make is that they don't listen to the advice of their expatriates once they come home. According to a survey by the Center for Global Assignments, 61 percent of employees who returned from overseas postings said they lacked opportunities to put their experience abroad to work at their home base. Every year, thousands of executives arrive home from overseas assignments, only to leave their jobs in the hope of finding greener pastures, often at a sunk cost of $1 million or more that their employer invested in training and overseas expenses. Twenty-five percent leave within a year—and typically go over to the competition. In fact, in a survey co-sponsored by CIGNA International Expatriates Benefits, the National Foreign Trade Council, and World at Work, employers responded that nearly half (49 percent) of returning expats leave their company within two years of repatriation. And in one extreme case, a company lost every one of the twenty-five managers it had sent on international assignments within one year of their return. The cost, found by J. Stewart Black and Hal B. Gregerson in a Harvard Business Review article: $50 million. "It might just as well have written a check for $50 million and tossed it to the winds."[23]

Despite the evidence, why are companies not treating repatriation seriously? A KPMG study showed that 23 percent of respondent companies start planning for the return of their expats only three months in advance, and a full 21 percent say they don't plan at all.[24]

Your Culture Clash

Before we go to the next chapter, take a few minutes right now and think of something you really want—an objective that "forces" you to work across cultures. (I am aware that many people skip over these types of questions. Don't be one of them. Invest the few minutes it takes to answer these questions. It will make *Culture Clash 2* a worthwhile investment of your time.)

Lab: Leadership-In-Action.

What business imperative or objective do you have that would require a breakthrough in working across borders or departments? _____

_____

_____

_____

_____

What is missing in your intercultural leadership for meeting this objective? _____

_____
_____
_____
_____

What blockages (in and around you) will you need to transcend to meet the objective? _____

_____
_____
_____
_____

What opportunities could you take advantage of to meet the objective? _____

_____
_____
_____
_____

What recurring chronic issue have you faced vis-à-vis your colleagues, buyers, suppliers, or alliance partners in working across borders or departments? _____

_____
_____
_____
_____

What is missing in your intercultural leadership for meeting this objective? _____

_____
_____
_____
_____
_____

What blockages (in and around you) will you need to transcend to meet the objective? _____

_____

_____

_____

_____

What opportunities could you take advantage of to meet the objective? _____

_____

_____

_____

_____

_____

Chapter Two

A New Leadership Landscape: Global Is In, National Is Out

*A significant portion of humanity thus finds itself on the
brink of an entirely new era in human affairs....The failure
of the totalitarian experiments coincided with the
awakening of humankind on a truly global scale.*

Zbigniew Brzezinski

What is heaven in Europe? It is a place with a German mechanic, a French lover, a British policeman, and an Italian cook. Now what is hell in Europe? Hell in Europe is a place with a French mechanic, an Italian policeman, a British cook, and finally, a German lover.

(The Germans would have you believe that hell is a place with a Swiss lover, but on behalf of Swiss lovers everywhere, I strenuously object.)

Jokes aside, where did this strong identification of character traits with national cultures come from? Why do many people tend to agree that "the French" make for great lovers but for so-so mechanics, and the Germans vice versa, even though that is likely baloney and such generalizations are often not borne out by the facts? After all, the nation-state has been the norm and primary actor in international relations only since 1648—the Peace of Westphalia—while transnational organizations existed many centuries ago and globalization is a new label for a fact older than nations. Take the Roman Empire and the Catholic Church.

Rome was a multicultural, multiethnic imperial super-state that spanned several continents. The Church, especially before the Lutheran and Zwinglian Reformations, was a super-state that commanded immense economic might and capital assets, military strength for crusades, cultural and ideological power, and enormous manpower. Church agents were an influence in virtually every kingdom, fiefdom, and township.

But for many centuries, in fact well into the twentieth, people did not think of themselves as global citizens. As late as 1941, Rebecca West wrote in her 1,200-page study of Yugoslavia that she had lain in a London hospital bed in October 1934 when she had heard on the radio that "the King of Yugoslavia had been assassinated in the streets of Marseille that morning."

> *I rang for my nurse, and when she came I cried to her, "Switch on the telephone! I must speak to my husband at once. A most terrible thing has happened. The King of Yugoslavia has been assassinated." "Oh, dear!" she replied. "Did you know him?" "No," I said. "Then why," she asked, "do you think it's so terrible?"*[25]

Times have changed since then. Only a few decades later, people the world over mourned the deaths of Princess Diana, King Hussein of Jordan, Michael Jackson, or Whitney Houston instantly and intimately as if they had been family members. In 2001, millions around the world watched in horror as three hijacked planes crashed into the World Trade Center and the Pentagon, and laid wreaths and lit candles in faraway cities for the 2,700 who had perished. In less than a century, human beings have gone from being defined by national borders to being members of a global citizenry.

Managers are part of the trend, too. In a *Forbes* article, the late management expert Peter Drucker declared obsolete one of his core assumptions: that national boundaries define the ecology of enterprise and management. Drucker defined a new reality in a phrase that I cited at the beginning of this book and bears repeating: "Management and national boundaries are no longer congruent. The scope of management can no longer be politically defined. National boundaries will continue to be important but as restraints on the practice of management, not in defining the practice."[26] Most managers work in a turbulent global market where one action in subprime mortgages in Florida can unleash a financial crisis that affects organizations and individuals everywhere.

Never before in history have humans dealt with humans from so many different cultures. Most of us meet people from other cultures every day. Even the fruit vendor on the street corner is tied up with the global market. Whether we like it or not, we are all global citizens. Globalization is both good and bad news—good because it presents us with new opportunities and bad because it challenges our assumptions about what it means to be human. In this global environment, expertise in collaborating with people from different cultures must be part of the skill-set of leaders at all levels and in all sectors of society. More than ever before, leadership now means taking a global perspective, synthesizing viewpoints, and collaborating across a wide spectrum of cultures. But extraordinary leaders in recent history—Gandhi and Churchill, Havel and Mandela, Kennedy and King, and also Jack Welch and Steve Jobs, Larry Page and Carlos Ghosn—have always lifted their gaze beyond their national borders to include the globe.

In the last generation, our experience of our global identity has been altered beyond what our grandparents could have imagined in their wildest dreams. The factors that have brought about this transformation include:

- The rise of the BRICS (Brazil, Russia, India, China and most recently South Africa), to use the acronym coined by Jim McNeill, as economic powerhouses.

- The shrinking of communication and transportation costs, the growth of international migration, and the emergence of the virtual team.

- The rise of capitalism, the rise of global media (including social media like Facebook, LinkedIn, and Twitter—or their European and Asian cousins Xing, Viadeo, and Renren), and the Americanization of global culture.
- The rise of international organizations and multinational corporations and the end of industry specificity.

Together, these transformations have utterly transformed the landscape in which today's leaders must operate. Let's briefly examine each.

BRICS and Emerging Markets

Foreign direct investment by Western companies continues— BP's $7.2 billion purchase of a 30 percent stake in India's offshore oil and gas fields of Reliance Industries is just one recent example. But in the last few years, a new phenomenon has changed the game: the BRICS countries—Brazil, Russia, India and China, and since 2010 South Africa—whose middle classes are growing quickly and whose companies now make their own large-scale acquisitions. According to the UN Population Division and Goldman Sachs, China alone is projected to boast a middle class of some 1.4 billion consumers by 2030 (currently around 300 million Chinese have discretionary incomes to buy items that were impossible a little over a decade ago). India will have the second largest middle class, with 1.07 billion moving up the income ladder, while Europe and the United States' middle classes will be 414 million and 365 million respectively.[27]

But we need not look twenty years from now. JuxtConsult, a New Delhi research firm, estimates that in 2010, 10 million Indians bought something online; in 2011 that number rose to 17 million. American online retailers have taken note. As of this writing, Amazon is building a warehouse and hiring employees for an Indian site, and Groupon has bought an Indian Web site, SoSasta.com.[28]

   The future began in 2009 when China became the world's largest automobile market. Car sales rose steadily after the government started issuing tax rebates for small engines. Western companies are getting more and more of their revenues from China. Yum! Brands generates about a third of its revenue from its KFC and Pizza Hut sales in China alone.[29] At the same time, China's retail sales are still growing at a double-digit rate despite the global financial turmoil. In the U.S., soft drink consumption in 2011 declined to its lowest level since 1996. Yet for the second quarter 2012 Coke reported plans to invest $4 billion in China, its business having doubled in that country alone in the previous five years.[30] It is obvious that China can no longer be considered an emerging market for many brands—rather it is swiftly becoming *the* market. Chinese companies have used this momentum to move aggressively into Europe and North America. The Zhejiang Geely Holding Group, China's largest private carmaker, paid $1.8 billion for Sweden's Volvo in 2010. In the United States, 2010 was the year in which 40 Chinese companies had U.S. Initial Public Offerings. And the Chinese are buying struggling Japanese companies: in 2011, the Chinese company Haier bought the washing machine and refrigerator business of Sanyo Electric for ¥10 billion ($124 million). That year, for the first time on record, the number of M&As by Chinese companies in Japan exceeded those by American businesses in the country.[31] That was also the year when the former powerhouse Japan faced a new reality: China had surpassed it as the world's second-largest economy.

   Indian companies have aggressively moved into cross-border acquisitions of their own as they hunt for new areas of growth. During the last decade the Tata Group, India's largest conglomerate, quietly purchased major Western brands such as Tetley Tea, the Ritz-Carlton and Pierre hotels, the Starwood Group hotel chain, Citigroup Global Services, Jaguar and Land Rover.[32] In 2010, Bharti Airtel, the Indian telecom giant, bought Zain Africa for $9 billion, bolstering its presence in fifteen African countries like Kenya and Nigeria. In 2011, the Essar Group, an Indian energy and steel conglomerate, made a bold acquisition: a British oil refinery from Shell for $350 million. "An asset at a good price is always worth looking at," said Prashant Ruia, Essar's chief executive, with quiet confidence, "as long as it fits into the overall strategy of our growth plan." Finally, the Adani Group purchased the Abbott Point port in Australia to ship coal to its power plants in India. Pricetag: $2 billion.[33]

Brazil has produced its own *Wirtschaftswunder*. Massive oil finds have created a powerful national exuberance and further bolstered the country's unquenchable self-belief. In the spring of 2012, talk in Rio was all about the offshore oil, the skyrocketing real estate, the 2014 World Cup, the 2016 Olympics, the proposed Rio-Sao Paulo high-speed rail, and the crazy prices (a plate of spaghetti for $60, anyone?). Brazil recently overtook Britain as the world's sixth-largest economy.

The new Brazilian confidence is felt as far as New York City. My friend Marcos Cohen, a Brazilian real estate broker at Prudential Douglas Elliman, said he had closed more than fifteen deals over the past two years for Brazilians paying from $5 million to more than $15 million for Manhattan apartments. According to Jeisa Chiminazzo, a Brazilian model who bought a two-bedroom loft in TriBeCa in 2009 for $1.65 million, the Brazilian invasion has at least one downside. "If you want to gossip a little bit, you can't gossip in Portuguese anymore," she said, "because you will have a Brazilian bump into you."[34]

Hence, what to some is a disaster, to others is a dream. While the West struggled through the 2007–2009 U.S. recession, the BRICS became the engines of the global economy for a time; they produced some 85 percent of world economic growth.[35] (To be sure, China, India, and Brazil slowed down in 2011 after raising their interest rates to fight inflation, but they were still growing faster than the U.S. and European economies.) Already by 2006, 58 of the Fortune 500 companies were headquartered in emerging markets.[36] In *Forbes'* 2011 list of the world's billion-aires, 108 of the 214 new names—more than half—added to the list came from Brazil, Russia, India, or China.

We may have to learn some new names, for example those of China's business elite, called "black collar class" for their black business suits and black limousines: Wang Jianzhou, who owns China Mobile, with 650 million subscribers the largest telecom network in the world; or Li Xiaolin, the electricity baron(ess) and chief of China Power International who provides power to over a billion people, the lone woman among China's most influential business people; and Xiao Gang, the boss of the Bank of China and of the Bank of China (Hong Kong), a rising star in China's politics.[37] Not to speak of the world's richest man, a Mexican, Carlos Slim, who is worth $74 billion and has pulled far ahead of his closest rivals Bill Gates ($56 billion) and Warren Buffett ($50 billion).[38]

Communication, Transportation, Migration, Virtual Teams

For much of history, only a tiny elite ever traveled more than walking distance from where they were born; now the average person has a sense of the nearness of other lands and the world as a whole. The Internet and the deregulation of telecoms have dramatically reduced the cost of long-distance communication. Close to 87 percent of the world population now has a mobile phone. Exchange of information with people almost anywhere in the world has become easier, faster, and cheaper than it ever was for previous generations. (Note, though, that most people in the world do not benefit from these lower costs. Three-quarters of Europeans use the Internet, and Internet use in emerging markets has soared by 4,000 percent in the last decade, but only every eighth person in Africa enjoys access.[39] An American needs to save one month's salary to buy a computer; a Bangladeshi must save eight years to do so.[40])

Because distance is no longer an obstacle, relationships once difficult to maintain are now commonplace. I regularly call colleagues or clients worldwide via Voiceover IP phones, or I Skype (yes, that is now a verb) them for free, using the screen-share feature to collaborate as if they were sitting beside me and looking at my computer monitor. I email them contracts or entire books. One result of these low communication costs is the rise of the virtual team, a team whose members rarely, if ever, meet in person. (The book you're reading now is a result of virtual collaboration among people in the United States, Europe, and Asia.) An extreme example happened in September 2001, when a team of surgeons in New York City performed a successful operation on a patient 4,500 miles away—in Strasbourg, France.

The virtual team is not a new phenomenon, though. In the past, if you were a traveling salesman or a CIA operative, you might work independently in the field and not see your boss for months at a time. As a radio announcer, you might get together with the program director only once a fortnight. But the PDA, the Web and cloud computing allow people to work from home or the beach, and make it possible for programmers in India to telecommute daily to jobs in California's Silicon Valley. Increasing technological complexity forces companies in high-tech industries to be global in order to keep pace with change. Companies may need to make use of lower wages or standards in emerging markets. And they may find themselves between a rock and a hard place when consumers demand low-cost devices and activists demand the upholding of standards or the safeguarding of jobs in the home country. Apple was in the news in the last two years over its use of Foxconn and other Chinese companies to assemble its iPhones and iPads after a wave of suicides and other deaths from an explosion at Foxconn. Managerial salaries in India or China are already or will soon be at the level of U.S salaries; but wages of Chinese or Indian manufacturing or bench-level scientists are between one-seventh and one-twelfth the salary an employee earns in the United States or Germany.

One American telecom is taking advantage of low rates by using customer service reps in Bangalore, India, who pose as Americans with American names, trained to speak in American accents with American customers. "Hi, my name is Susan Sanders, and I'm from Chicago," a twenty-two-year-old introduces herself with a broad smile and even broader vowels. In fact, "Susan Sanders" is C.R. Suman, a native of Bangalore who fields calls from customers in the United States. Just in case her callers ask personal questions, Ms. Suman has created a fictional biography, complete with her parents Bob and Ann, brother Mark and a made-up business degree from the University of Illinois. Her training by Customer Assets, the calling center, included listening to sitcoms like "Ally McBeal" or "Friends" without the picture and then reconstructing the dialogue and being quizzed by the trainer, who would pose as a caller, on American movies, sports, and television programs. The point of the pretense is to convince Americans that the person on the other end of the line works right nearby—not 8,300 miles away. Companies like General Electric or British Airways have set up supermarket-size phone banks in cities like Bangalore or Haiderabad to handle a huge volume of daily customer inquiries. India is attractive because of its widespread use of English and its low-cost labor.

Indian call-centers serving U.S. customers are only the low end of a huge and growing industry of cross-border virtual teams including Indian software developers, transcribers, accountants, web designers, and animation artists. "India is on its way to being the back office for the world," says Shriram Ramdas, co-founder of Bangalore Labs, which manages Web sites and information networks for companies from the outskirts of Bangalore. While their American clients sleep, Indian software writers churn out code, which is then beamed by satellite to the United States.

These companies are highly pragmatic and care little about the national identity we saw at the beginning of this chapter.

Subroto Bagchi, a partner in an Indian software firm, said: "We see ourselves as a next-generation company that is neither Indian nor American."[41] The results speak for themselves: by 2010, Business Process Outsourcing (BPO) had become a $12.4 billion industry, and India its leading star, cornering some 80 percent of that market, but other outsourcing regions were catching up, especially Eastern Europe (Czech Republic, Hungary, Russia, Poland), Asia (China, Malaysia, Philippines), and Mexico and South Africa. NBC attracted seven million viewers with its sitcom "Outsourced" about a Kansas City company that moves jobs to a call center in India and sends a U.S. manager there to head the operation.[42]

Transportation is also easier and cheaper today than ever. In 1900, traveling from New York City to London took usually six days and cost a fortune. Today, a flight from New York to London takes seven hours and as little as five hundred dollars. Needless to say, many more people are now able to travel, and those who do, travel much farther and more often than they did in the past.

Lower transportation costs enhance international mobility and migration. According to the World Bank, the number of migrants worldwide had more than doubled to 215 million people between 1992 and 2010—roughly one out of every thirty humans is on the move today.[43] People migrate for many reasons: to flee political repression, escape poverty, seek economic opportunity, or join loved ones. Whatever the reasons, transnational migration has changed the face of societies. In some neighborhoods in the Swiss cities Basel or Zurich, up to 80 percent of students in primary schools are now from abroad—from countries like Bosnia, Turkey, Lebanon, Senegal—because of Switzerland's relatively liberal immigration policy.

The current Euro crisis has Germany looking to southern and eastern Europe for educated but desperate—and desperately needed—workers. German companies have recruited thousands of workers from Poland and Romania, but increasingly from crisis-stricken Greece, and from Italy, Portugal, and

Spain. In 2011 the German population grew for the first time since 2002 thanks to a net immigration of 240,000 people, nearly double the 128,000 net gain the year before. This leads to culture clashes, and not just because of xenophobic skinheads. Many Spaniards said working in Germany takes getting used to, with Germans far more direct and much quieter. No one makes personal phone calls during business hours, but the workday is much shorter. They were surprised that they were expected to greet coworkers each morning with handshakes and to call them "Herr" and "Frau." Germans cut off hallway conversations over work issues, suggesting it would be more appropriate to schedule a formal meeting. The German fondness for order, often joked about, was true, said Carlos Baixeras, a thirty-year-old engineer near Frankfurt. "There are rules for everything," he said. "There is a trash police."[44]

Driven by international migration, many of today's children are so-called Third Culture Kids (TCKs), a term coined already in the 1950s by Ruth Hill Useem for children who accompany their parents into another society. Hanah Lee, a teenage girl interviewed for a video on TCKs, was asked what she considers home. Her answer: "So I am Korean-American and I was born and raised in New Jersey for a few years, and then when I was nine I moved to Japan, and then when I was twelve I moved to Guatemala, so there are a couple of different places I called home." The multiplicity of languages in Ms. Lee's family at times led to awkward moments: "I had a Korean-American friend visit once and it was just me and my mom and this Korean-American friend, and we were all having this conversation and switching between Korean and English really easily, and then my mom and I were suddenly switching to Japanese without even realizing. And it happens all the time when we're together but we kind of forget that we have to live with ourselves around other people, and so my friend was just sitting there for like a good five minutes, chuckling nervously and going, 'I don't know what's happening.'"[45]

Back in Europe, in the Cremona province of the Italian Po Valley, alongside common local last names like Ferrari or Galli, a new name has become more and more common: Singh. For the past twenty years, Indian immigrants from the Punjab have settled in Italy's agricultural heartland that produces about one-tenth of Italy's milk, often as *bergamini* or dairy workers. Nearly 16,000 Indians are legally employed in Italy's agriculture, and according to one estimate, about one-third of the 3,000 agricultural laborers in Cremona are Indian. "Young Italians don't want to work those kinds of hours," said Mayor Dalido Malaggi of Pessina Cremonese.[46] Some people say that if the Indian workers went on strike, production of *Grana Padano,* the hard grainy cheese that is the specialty of this region, would shut down.

Americanization, Media, Social Media

The breakdown of the former Communist states has compounded an "Americanization" of global culture. The world has embraced capitalism, which is seeping even into former socialist diehards like China or Cuba (North Korea seems to be the lone holdout) and is pushing many millions of new consumers and producers into the global economy. In 2011 almost 50 percent of the Fortune 500 revenues came from outside the USA;[47] the year before, a full 60 percent of Nike's earnings came from emerging markets.[48] The common demand of the popular uprisings in Tunisia, Syria, Libya, and Bahrain is that they all asked for an equal share in the fruits of free enterprise. There is now one Western model of consumption, for better or for worse. And wherever people live, they clamor pretty much for the same brands. Influenced by Hollywood films that reach all the corners of the world, by Western-style advertising, by CNN and MTV, people the world over tend to have more and more uniform tastes. They Google, smoke Marlboros, listen to Rihanna or Red Hot Chili Peppers, or watch House. If you ask kids in Gaza for their favorite movies, they say "Rambo." J. R. of "Dallas" fame is a revered icon on billboards in Bulgaria. And Osama Bin Laden, the terror organization Al Qaeda's late leader, was in love with the late soul diva Whitney Houston and was rumored to have drawn up expensive plans to assassinate her former husband Bobby Brown.

The global flow of information, people, goods, and money has accelerated to such an extent that it seems as though the world has shrunk (Citigroup alone moves some $3 trillion around the world each day, and former CEO Vikram Pandit reportedly said if Citi were allowed to unravel, "100 governments around the world would be trying to figure out how to pay their employees"[49]). In turn, by seemingly shrinking the world, super-fast communication and transportation have altered our experience of time: it seems to be speeding up. Some call this phenomenon Internet time: one Internet year equals four months. When the American colonies proclaimed their Declaration of Independence from Great Britain, it took several weeks for the news to reach England. It now happens instantaneously and can be watched on a video feed. When the United States-led coalition declared war on Iraq, Saddam Hussein reportedly watched the event live on CNN.

Twenty years later, during the Arab Spring, dictators in the Middle East could follow their own demise live on Facebook or Twitter—in English or in their own language. English accounts for only 31 percent of languages used online, so a social media campaign could easily miss vast segments of the global market. Facebook figures show that English is the most used language on Facebook, followed by Spanish, French, Turkish, and Indonesian. And social networks like LinkedIn or Youtube are not the only ones. Social media of all stripes have created vast communities of people who share their lives and watch each other virtually. In Europe, it's Xing or Viadeo; in China it's the massively popular Qzone or Renren, used by 380 million and 120 million customers respectively; in Japan it's Mixi, with about 30 million users; and Orkut in India and Brazil.

There are significant differences in how people in different cultures use social media. Forrester Research found, for example, that Chinese city-dwellers who go online are three times more likely to visit a social network than the Japanese; that 69 percent of European social media users (and even 73 percent of U.S. users) are "spectators" who read blogs or tweets, watch videos, or listen to podcasts; that only 23 percent in Europe (and 24 percent in the United States) are "creators" who publish a blog or website, upload media, or post articles. The picture is very different in India and China, where more than two-thirds of online adults are "creators" who produce and post social content.[50] Marketers have to be cognizant of this new landscape.

Multinational Corporations, International Organizations

It all goes to show that the unprecedented concentration of world media in the hands of just a few—Rupert Murdoch, AOL/Time Warner, and the BBC—compounds this growing uniformity of tastes. And this brings up our final driver of the new landscape that comes with global capitalism: the rise of global corporations. Multinationals *per se* are not a new phenomenon. Fiat, General Motors, and several European insurance companies were multinational entities already in the nineteenth or early twentieth century. What *is* new is their stunning growth in recent decades. Yahoo produces more annual revenue than Mongolia; if eBay were a country, it would be bigger than Madagascar; Walmart makes more money than Norway, the twenty-fifth largest economy in the world.[51]

The national identity of multinationals can be a confusing matter, since production processes too have become global. The "Japanese" company Toyota is one of the larger employers in the United States. It produces cars with American workers, American management, and American parts. Should Toyota still be seen as a Japanese firm? Mabuchi Motor controls over half the world market in mini-motors for zoom lenses, toothbrushes, and car windows, and employs 36,000 workers, only 736 of whom live in Japan. "United States" companies are similar: in 2010, Coca-Cola reported 70 percent of its revenues from outside the United States. A full 60 percent of Nike's earnings came from emerging markets.[52] Over 40 percent of the market for Coca-Cola, Gillette, Lucent, Boeing, and GE power systems is in Asia.[53] Even the stalwart American company General Motors (which in 2010 sold more cars and trucks in China than in the United States[54]) produces 40 percent of its cars beyond American shores. Of the company's 252,000 employees, 152,000 work abroad, building Chevrolets, Opels, Vauxhalls, Holdens, and Buicks in 33 different countries.[55] The company is as multinational as each of its cars. Whether GM is still an American firm is doubtful.[56]

Given their global infrastructure and marketing, companies need truly global management. Diversity is becoming a fact of life within the top management teams of multinational corporations. In 1998, the late C. K. Prahalad and Kenneth Lieberthal predicted that by 2010, over one-third of board members of multinationals would be people from China, India, and Brazil, since those countries would be the most populated and fastest-growing markets with the largest middle classes. The authors asserted that businesses would run into trouble unless they diversified their management early on.[57] While we don't know if Prahalad and Lieberthal's prediction has been borne out by reality (to my knowledge there is no comprehensive data on the makeup of Fortune 500 boards), the ascent of chiefs from emerging markets is undeniable: Anshu Jain at Deutsche Bank, Vikram Pandit at Citi, Indra Nooyi at Pepsico, Carlos Brito at Inbev, Hikmet Ersek at Westner Union, and Francisco D'Souza at Cognizant are just the more prominent examples of a rising trend.

The emergence of international institutions in the second half of the twentieth century also had a profound effect on globalization. The General Agreement on Tariffs and Trade and its successor, the World Trade Organization, lowered trade barriers around the world. World trade increased from $308 billion in 1950 to over 15 trillion by 2010 (although taking a serious 12 percent hit in the crisis year 2009).[58] The World Bank and the International Monetary Fund dictate economic policies in Turkey, Tajikistan, and Togo. The European Union has become a regulatory super-state with its own flag and courts, legislature and executive, central bank and currency, impacting the lives of all citizens in all member states (seventeen of the twenty-seven EU members belong to the Eurozone). The claim that the days of the nation-state are numbered is certainly a vast exaggeration, but it is undeniable that many of the mega issues facing the nation state—from AIDS to the environment, trade to terrorism—transcend the nation-state's scope of action and require a new level of multilateral cooperation. The proliferation of international organizations and the delegation of more and more competencies to them are the predictable response.[59]

*   *   *

Globalization can be good news if it leads to better understanding and greater harmony among cultures. Or it can be bad if local tastes or preferences are obliterated in favor of super-brands like MTV, Madonna, and McDonald's, which dominate by virtue of their superior marketing muscle; or if we have become interconnected to such a degree that investors everywhere tremble at a credit crisis in the United States, the economy in Japan following the Fukushima nuclear accident, or the Euro crisis. For better or worse, we now live in a world in which the proverbial butterfly that flaps its wings in Bangkok can in fact unleash a storm in California.

Some argue that the globalization trend is countered by opposite trends.[60] In response to the growing homogenization of humanity, they point to growing nationalism, ethnic division, and "tribalism," which hold many areas of the world in their grip. One example is military power: According to the International

Institute for Strategic Studies in London, China expanded from two Soviet-era destroyers in 1990 to thirteen modern destroyers in 2010.[61] Another are separatist movements around the world, from Azerbaijan (Nagomo-Karabakh) to Chechnya to Tibet,

Others warn that at the very time when barriers to communication and travel and trade have come down and we make contact with more people in more places, we feel less and less connected. They say that the concept of the "individual," which was a powerful invention in the eighteenth century, is getting out of hand; the cult of individualism and the free market has led to diminished relationships and to isolation—to a "you or me" world. There are those who seek to return to traditional values. In South Korea, for example, the word "Confucian" has long been synonymous with "old-fashioned." But Park Seok-hong, chief curator of the country's oldest private Confucian academy, and others like him have gained—with their campaign to reawaken interest in Confucian teachings focusing on communal harmony, respect for seniority, and loyalty to the state—principles that many older Koreans believe have lost their grip on the young. Since 2007, a steadily growing number of schoolchildren, as many as 15,000 a year, have come here for a course on Confucian etiquette. "I came here so Grandpa will scold me less," explained Kang Ku-hyun, a sixth-grader from Seoul.[62]

Whether the forces of globalism or those of tribalism will win out, coordinating activities worldwide is infinitely more complex for firms than it used to be to manage within the same nation. Managing across borders faces you with seemingly insurmountable issues—cultural, political, technical, or communicative. Non-tariff barriers, standards, and laws impede commerce between countries, and state subsidies of certain industries make competition difficult. There are national differences—different tastes or languages, different media or practices.

At the most mundane level, cultures may have different speeds. For example, the rhythm of a typical Swedish movie is much slower than that of an American movie, but still too fast for Indian viewers. Some Indian movies are so slow that you might learn meditation just by watching. So when your IT people build a website, they need to be cognizant of the fact that visitors will likely be people from vastly different value systems. If you play flash video, remember that U.S. visitors might be used to much faster, MTV-style visuals than people from, say, Sweden or India. (This example is not trivial: if global companies want to reach the key markets of the twenty-first century, the growing Indian middle class is a larger audience than the entire population of the United States or even Europe.)

Chapter Three

Leading through Language: What Do You Speak?

A man who is ignorant of other languages is ignorant of his own.
Johann Wolfgang von Goethe

The bus stops and two Italian men get on. They sit down and engage in an animated conversation. The lady sitting in front of them ignores them at first, but her attention is galvanized when she hears one of the men say the following: "Emma come first. Den I come. Den two asses come together. I come once-a-more. Two asses, they come together again. I come again and pee twice. Then I come one lasta time."

"You foul-mouthed swine," retorts the lady indignantly. "In this country we don't talk about our sex lives in public!"

"Hey, coola down lady," says the man. "Whosa talkin' abouta sex? I'm justa tellin' my friend how to spella 'Mississippi'!"[63]

The Power of Cultural Mindsets

This joke, like most at the outset of each chapter, shows what can go wrong in cross-cultural interactions. We have a filter through which we hear what's being said, and things can easily get lost in translation. The lady in the bus *knew* what the two Italians were talking about. Of course they were talking about dirty sex, and she never once stopped to check her own assumptions before lashing out. Her brain was wired to accept only one reality, one perspective. And that is what this chapter is about: how does our language shape what we can see or hear—and how we perceive our reality and the world?

I must confess that I fell prey to a similar misunderstanding once (and who knows how many other times, when my interlocutors were merely too polite to point it out to me). In a previous incarnation, back in 1986, I was named the global manager of an international education campaign involving twenty-seven countries. On a conference call with the organization's president, I laid out the whole structure, including management by time zones and national campaign managers. The president was impressed and complimented me for the design and preparation. Then I described how excited people around the world were about the campaign—that's when I committed the gaffe. I was twenty-four at the time, I ran the campaign from the Munich office, and my English was good but not perfect. Especially slang expressions were beyond me. What I meant to say was, "Everybody is really turned on by the campaign." What came out of my mouth was, "Everybody is really horny."

There was a pause on the other end that lasted several seconds but seemed excruciatingly long. Nobody said anything. Then finally the President said, "Thomas, that sounds wonderful." Upon which everyone on the call hung up only too quickly. I knew that I had done something wrong—but what? A senior staffer in the global office called me a few minutes later to say that the president was thrilled with my strategic thinking. Then she said: "Do me a favor: don't ever say on a conference call that everybody is horny, okay?"

Since we are on the topic, let's talk about sex some more which, needless to say, is not talked about with the same openness in every culture. "Most Egyptians are secretive about sex," Aliaa Magda Elmahdy told CNN, "because they are brought up thinking sex is something bad and dirty, and there is no mention of it in schools." Elmahdy had set off a wave of outrage in 2011 when, in a perhaps ill-considered attempt to promote sexual equality and free expression in Egypt after the Arab Spring, she posted nude photos of herself online.

She may have a kindred spirit in the United States: Gary Chapman, a seventy-three-year-old Southern Baptist pastor and author of *Five Love Languages* which has sold over seven million copies. "That is the idea that good Christians don't talk about sex," Chapman told a crowd of 1,000 at a conference in a church outside Nashville, Tennessee. "At least not out loud, and certainly not in the church." He may have a point. In a video called "No Second Chances" that is used in abstinence-only courses in the United States, a student asks a school nurse, "What if I want to have sex before I get married?" To which the nurse replies, "Well, I guess you'll just have to be prepared to die."

Swedish culture discusses sex entirely differently. In her 2006 book, *When Sex Goes to School,* Kristin Luker told of visiting sex-education classes in Sweden and hearing an instructor's response to the question, "What is an orgasm, and why do people talk about it so much?" The teacher's response: "Orgasm is the moment of highest pleasure during sex, and that's why people talk about it so much."[64]

Or take the related topic of privacy. Max Schrems, a twenty-four-year-old law student in Salzburg, Austria, wanted to know how much Facebook knew about him, and requested his own Facebook file. What he got turned out to be a virtual *Bildungsroman* of 1,222 pages, containing wall posts he had deleted, old messages that revealed a friend's troubled state of mind, even information he had never entered himself about his physical whereabouts.

Mr. Schrems felt a vague unease about what Facebook might do with all that information. "It's like a camera hanging over your bed while you're having sex. It just doesn't feel good," he said. "We in Europe are oftentimes frightened of what might happen some day."

He is far from alone. In Japan and Switzerland, Google was widely criticized for being intrusive when its self-driven cars cruised the streets with a camera snapping pictures for Google Street View. According to the *New York Times,* it's worse: when

Google's cars drive by your house, they apparently scoop up your most private emails too. "It was one of the biggest violations of data protection laws that we had ever seen," Johannes Caspar, a German data protection official, told the *Times* after he forced Google to show him what its Street View cars had been collecting from his fellow citizens. "We were very angry."

This might be a clash of European vs. American values. "In the United States, privacy is a consumer business," Jacob Kohnstamm, chairman of the Dutch Data Protection Authority, told the *Times.* "In Europe, it is a fundamental rights issue."[65]

In other cultures, people might transgress the boundaries of privacy without a second thought. In India, a shopkeeper might casually ask a childless woman if she has gynecological trouble, school grades are posted on public walls, and many people still live in extended families, literally wandering in and out of each other's bedrooms. Only recently, a government project to issue biometric identity cards to every Indian citizen set off a flurry of concern, prompting the government to draft a law that enshrines the right to privacy—for the first time in India's history.[66]

It all comes down to language: the vastly different meanings for words like "sex" or "privacy" in different cultural contexts can get lost in translation. To take another example, the word "promise" or "commitment" can have vastly different meanings in different cultural contexts depending on whether they are uttered (or heard) in a Lutheran culture, like the Netherlands or Scandinavia, where people tend to be careful what they promise because they would feel guilty for not delivering on the promise; or in a Catholic culture, like Italy or Brazil where you get absolution for breaking your word; or in a culture like the United States, where making promises tends to be more like a tool for playing a large-scale game and reaching beyond what's predictable.

These different meanings can even live side by side in the same person. One result of globalization is that more and more children grow up in bilingual families and multilingual surroundings. My daughter Hannah, who is a dual American and Swiss citizen like me, is an example of that. At the age of two, she said bilingual things like "Daddy, isch das dini watch?" or "Come on baby, mir ässed äs Gummibärli."

As we have seen, a Turkish girl might go to school in Berlin and speak Turkish at home and German in school. Even if she does not go on to study in London and fall in love with a Frenchman, recent studies have shown a significant difference between the brains of monolingual babies who hear only one language at home, and bilingual babies who hear two. Researchers at the University of Washington found that at six months, the monolingual infants could still distinguish between phonetic sounds, whether in the language they were used to hearing or in another language not spoken in their homes. But as they grew to ten or twelve months, the monolingual babies were no longer detecting sounds in the second language, only in the language they usually heard. In contrast, the bilingual infants at ten to twelve months were able to discriminate sounds in both languages.

"What the study demonstrates is that the variability in bilingual babies' experience keeps them open," said Dr. Patricia Kuhl, co-director of the Institute for Learning and Brain Sciences at the University of Washington and a co-author of the study. "They do not show the perceptual narrowing as soon as monolingual babies do. It's another piece of evidence that what you experience shapes the brain."[67] If we take that statement to its logical conclusion, different languages might even lead to different brain structures.

At the very least, it seems clear that our language and the way we look at the world are correlated and in a sort of dance with one another. But which way does the causal vector point? Does language shape reality (as in, "the Yellow Danger" or "Americans are bullies") or is it the other way around (as in, China really is a danger and Americans really are bullies, we are only calling a spade a spade)? Be that as it may, new research at

MIT has shown that language is essential to being human. Language, says the anthropologist Mark Pagel, was instrumental in enabling social learning—our ability to acquire new behaviors that helped our evolution by watching and imitating others, which in turn accelerated our species on a trajectory of what anthropologists call "cumulative cultural evolution," a bustling of ideas successively building and improving on others.[68] Language was the crucial feature without which we might have never evolved from being Neanderthals.

Pagel's assertion is supported by experiments today. When language was taken away from people, they were no smarter than rats or infants. In one study, MIT students were asked to count dots on a screen. When they were allowed to count normally, they did great. When they had to do a non-linguistic task like banging out a rhythm while counting, they still did great. But when they had to simultaneously repeat a verbal text such as a news report while being shown the dots, they did poorly. They needed their language skills to count.[69]

All this goes to show that the languages we speak not only express or reflect our thoughts, but also shape the very thoughts we wish to (or are even able to) express. Our language shapes our reality. Or perhaps we should use the plural term: our languages shape our realities. If, as the German philosopher Martin Heidegger put it, language is the house of being—or Charlemagne more than a thousand years before him, who proclaimed that "To have a second language is to have a second soul"—then different languages shape different souls, different ways of being. Studies have confirmed that different languages shape the way you and I understand, think about, and experience "reality."

Patterns in language reveal hidden values, attitudes, and mindsets; in other words, culture. If I say, "Federer hit the ball," in English it is clear that he hit the ball in the past, not in the present, while in Indonesian, you need not—indeed, cannot—change the verb to mark the past tense. On the other hand, in

English it is not clear—except perhaps from the context— whether Roger Federer or his wife Mirka hit the ball (after all, she used to be a tennis pro too), while the Russian or Hebrew languages would make a clear distinction between a male and female ending of the verb. In Turkish, you have a different verb form depending on how you acquired the information about Federer hitting the ball. For example, you would use one verb form if you saw him hitting the ball with your own eyes, and another if you heard or read about the event second-hand.

In another investigation, Spanish and Japanese speakers could not remember the agents of accidental events as readily as English speakers could. Why? In Japanese and Spanish, the agent of causality is dropped: "The vase broke," rather than "John broke the vase."[70] In Spanish or Japanese, people later did not remember as well as English speakers who committed an accidental error such as popping a balloon, breaking an egg or spilling a drink.

This has profound consequences for how people assign responsibility for events, whether they blame each other, or if and how they punish each other. In a related study, English speakers watched the video of Janet Jackson's infamous "wardrobe malfunction" (a wonderful non-agentive coinage introduced into the English language by Justin Timberlake), accompanied by one of two written reports. The reports were identical, except in the last sentence where one report used the agentive phrase "ripped the costume" while the other said "the costume ripped." Even though everyone watched the same video and witnessed the ripping with their own eyes, language mattered. Not only did people who had read "ripped the cos-tume" blame Justin Timberlake more, they also levied a whop-ping 53 percent more in fines.[71]

The concept of agency brings us to leadership, for which not one universal definition exists either. Leadership has diverse connotations in different cultures. For example, in our male-dominated culture that has prevailed for several thousand years, many people associate leadership with forceful, over-bearing behavior or with command-and-control.

In German-speaking cultures, the word "leadership" would be translated as "Führerschaft"—not exactly a word people are at ease with. And Germans are not alone with their skepticism: as Rabbi Aaron Raskin and I write in our book *The Rabbi and the CEO,* Jewish scholars do "not approve of lordship, because . . . no mortal can lord over another . . ." Already the first-century Talmudic scholar Rabbi Yohanan cautioned, "Woe to leadership, for it buries those who possess it."[72] Both in Sweden and Japan, leadership is a lower priority than building consensus, and most people feel better if they can get by without sticking their necks out. Similarly, "there is a degree of skepticism in the UK towards anyone who tries to lead, and a belief in the inspired amateur which discourages people from having leadership roles," according to the director-general of the Institute of Directors in Britain. This reluctance to lead is reinforced by the British view that it is unseemly, and a bit cheap really, to blow your own horn. In the former Eastern Bloc countries, there is a marked reluctance to lead and take initiative, since under socialism, the state used to take charge of people's lives for so many years.

In Latin cultures, leaders are generally expected to be more autocratic and less participatory than in, say, U.S. or Scandinavian cultures. In the U.S. culture, the term leadership is used for just about anything that can be marketed and makes it sound better, from "leadership leases" to "leadership donors" to the "Democratic Leadership Council." Americans are often caught in the myth of "the faultless leader." Many of them like to believe in Camelot, the white knight who saves us from the mundane. Leaders must have a flawless character. If they are not super-human, they are discredited and soon discarded—unless they die first, in which case they live on in the imagination as forever young, dynamic, and pure. Those who survive are given a hard time; witness Bill Clinton or George W. Bush. (The jury is still out on Barack Obama.)

By the way, if you question the relevance language has for your business imperatives, think again. Language can profoundly influence the positioning of a product or service.

Best Practice: Building One Global Brand

Insigniam worked with a team at a Fortune 100 pharmaceutical producer of a leading over-the-counter (OTC) respiratory remedy. The medication enjoyed significant market share in the United States, but suffered from a myriad of divergent positioning and even formulations in different countries, resulting in its fragmented platform and its inability to leverage the global franchises. Not only was the corporate mindset different in each country, but the marketing was different. How can you have one global brand if each country pushes its own brand identity? For example, in the United States the drug was marketed as a decongestant; but "decongestant" does not even exist as a term in Germany, nor does the ailment "congestion." So Insigniam consultants interviewed each senior manager in each country and in each function to see where they could find a common language. Not an easy thing, since the team leader and coordinator was British and the team members were from all over the world.

And that was just the beginning. Once they got into the first work session, they found that one doctor in R&D had a vital contribution to make, but could not sell his ideas to the rest of the division because they discounted *anything* coming from R&D. Their first order of work was to give participants the opportunity to put their cross-cultural—and in this case cross-functional—perceptions and prejudices on the table. Once the team members had brought the different mindsets to light, they could unhook themselves from those mindsets and actually hear what the R&D doctor was proposing. The new strategies he showed his colleagues led the team to invent one common ambition: they chose to go after "nasal and respiratory health." This ambition then became the tree that could support different branches, as it were. The team was able to integrate the richness of each culture, which ultimately led to significant growth worldwide.

*   *   *

Or perhaps globalization has led to a merging of languages. The lexicographer Peter Sokolowski, editor at large for the Merriam-Webster archive, is in charge of finding new words in the media and seeing if they have become part of everyday language. One German word has been part of the (written) English language since 1895: *Schadenfreude,* "enjoyment obtained from the troubles of others" or literally the combination of "damage" and "joy." Lots of other German words have become indispensable to the English language. *Kindergarten, Angst, Poltergeist, Wanderlust, Pumpernickel, Fräulein, Bildungsroman, Lederhosen, verboten,* and *kaput* no longer need translation.[73] The same with French expressions: *à la carte, au contraire, au pair, avant garde, coup d'état, fait accompli, force majeure, joie de vivre, Mardi gras, raison d'être,* and *vis-à-vis.*

So perhaps a new breed of human being is beginning to exist, one who uses a *potpourri* (another French word) of languages and is at home anywhere in the world? This brings us to the next chapter, on global citizenship.

Chapter Four

Global Citizenship:
A Core Competence

I am a citizen, not of Athens or Greece, but of the world.
Socrates

We have seen that language gives us the lens through which we see the world. That lens can distort what we see. Do you know the one about the Italian who came to New York? (Apologies to our Italian friends, I realize this is already the second time we poke fun at them. But this joke is simply too good to pass up. Even my Italian sister-in-law thinks it's funny, and my mother-in-law asks me repeatedly to tell it at family dinners so perhaps you will let me get away with it too. I promise it will be the last time.)

"Ona day, I'ma go to New York, to a bigga hotel. I go down to hava soma breakfast. I tella the waitress I want two piss o toast. She branga me only one piss. I tella her I want two piss. She say, 'Go to the toilet.' I say, 'You no understand; I want two piss on my plate.' She say, 'You better not piss on your plate, you sonamabitch.' I don't even know the lady, and she calla me sonamabitch!

Later, I'ma go to Drake restaurant, very good restaurant. The waitress branga me a spoon an a knife, but no fock. I tella her I wanna fock. She say, 'Everybody wanna fock.' I tella her, 'No, no, you no understand; I wanna fock ona table.' She say, 'You better not fock on the table, you sonamabitch.' I don't even know the lady, and she calla me sonamabitch!

Finally, I'ma go back to my room ina hotel, and there's no sheet on my bed. I calla the manager. I say, 'I wanna sheet.' He say, 'Go to the toilet.' I say, 'No, no, no, you no understand. I wanna sheet on my bed.' He say, 'You better not sheet on your bed, you sonamabitch.' I don't even know the man, and he calla me sonamabitch!

I say, this is enough. I wanna go back to Italy. So I'ma go down to reception, and the man at reception, he say to me, 'Piss to you.' I say, 'Piss ona you too, you sonamabitch. I'ma go back to Italy.'"

Never mind the Italian. Let's talk about *your* global citizenship. Many years ago a participant in one of our workshops, Jim May of Dow Corning, told me a term executives and workers use in his company: the "Idiot Factor" means that the farther away people are from us, the more we think of them as idiots. (The Idiot Factor is at work not only in culture clashes, but also between divisions, for example R&D vs. sales or technical vs. non-technical people.) Some version of the Idiot Factor is at work always and anywhere, whether you are conscious of it or not. One way to counteract the Idiot Factor is seeing the world as a whole and the connections between things, as well as how others live around the world—essential vistas for leaders. Sometimes statistics can give us a picture of the world like nothing else can.

A Global Citizen's Mini-Briefing[74]

- World population: 7,011,672,189.
- Births per 1,000 population: 20. Deaths per 1,000 population: 8. Natural annual increase: 1.2 percent.
- Projected population in 2025: 8,084,000,000; in 2050: 9,587,000,000.
- Infant mortality rate (= infant deaths per 1,000 live births): 44. Highest IMR in the world: Afghanistan (131 per 1,000),

followed by Chad (125 per 1,000). Lowest IMR: Singapore (2 per 1,000).

- Humans under 15 years of age: 27 percent (in Africa, 41 percent). Humans over 65 years old: 8 percent (in Africa, 4 percent).

- Secondary school enrollment: 70 percent of males, 68 percent of females.

- Number of women who die annually from pregnancy-related causes: 529,000 (1 per minute).[75]

- Percentage of world food produced by women: 70 percent.[76]

- Per-capita Gross National Product worldwide: $10,240 per year. The highest are Luxembourg and Qatar with $113, 533 and $98,329 respectively. The lowest is in the Democratic Republic of Congo at $216.[77]

- Percentage of the world's income earned by the wealthiest quintile (20 percent of the world's population): 86 percent. Percentage owned by the poorest quintile: 1.1 percent.[78]

- Number of United Nations employees: 63,540. Number of employees at Coca-Cola: 74,000.[79]

- Annual UN peacekeeping operations budget (July 1, 2011, to June 30, 2012): $7.06 billion. Estimated cost of UN Peacekeeping operations from 1948 to June 2010: $69 billion.[80] World military spending (2010): $1.63 trillion.[81]

Another, perhaps even starker, way of looking at the world is to imagine that we can shrink its population to a village of 100 people, with all the existing human ratios remaining the same.[82] Here is (approximately) how such a village would look:

- 61 would be from Asia, 12 from Europe, 13 from the Americas, 13 from Africa, and one from Oceania.

- 52 would be female and 48 male; 90 would be heterosexual and 10 homosexual.

- 70 would be "of color" and 30 white, 33 Christian, 19 Muslim, 13 Hindu, 6 Buddhist, and 29 other or atheist.

- 6 people would possess 59 percent of the entire world's wealth, and all 6 would be from the United States.
- 80 people would live in substandard housing.
- 70 would be unable to read.
- 30 would regularly have enough to eat, and 70 would not.
- 48 could not speak or act according to their faith and conscience due to harassment, imprisonment, torture, or death.
- 1 would be near death; 2 near birth.
- 1 would have a college education.
- 7 would have a computer, 93 would not.
- 17 would speak Chinese, 9 English, 8 Hindi, 6 Spanish, 6 Russian, and 4 Arabic.

When one considers our world from such a compressed perspective, the need for mutual understanding and education becomes glaringly apparent. If you awoke this morning with more health than illness, you are better off than the one million people who will not survive this week. If you have never experienced the danger of battle, the loneliness of imprisonment, the agony of torture, or the pangs of starvation, you are ahead of 500 million people in the world. If you can attend a church (or mosque or synagogue or temple) meeting without fear of harassment, arrest, torture, or death, you are more blessed than three billion people in the world. If you have food in the refrigerator, clothes on your back, a roof overhead, and a place to sleep, you are richer than 75 percent of the world population. If you have money in the bank or in your wallet, and spare change in a dish somewhere, you are among the wealthiest eight percent of the world's people. And if you can read this book (a fairly safe bet), you are more advantaged than 17 percent of humanity who are illiterate.[83]

Lab.

This brief exercise is designed to acquaint you with how about one-quarter of humanity lives. All you need is a few moments and your imagination. Imagine yourself in your own house. Now take the television(s) out. Take away the refrigerator and freezer, the stove, the dishwasher, the microwave, the washing machine and dryer, the burglar alarm, and all other appliances. Instead, you have a small wood stove for cooking and heat. Now take away the heat. Take away safe drinking water. Take away your bed. Take away the other furniture. Take away electricity; you have candles. Take away all carpets; you have an earthen floor. Take away the bathroom; you have to go outside to relieve yourself and you wash yourself from a bucket of water. Now take away your house; you have a shack or hut with one room and a corrugated tin roof. When the sun is shining, it gets unbearably hot. When it rains, the roof leaks and all your possessions get damp.

Now imagine that you are a woman. You have five children and are pregnant again. You have had four years of schooling, more than most girls in your community. You get up before dawn to walk twenty miles to the neighboring village to get water and matches for the stove. The nearest school is there too. If your kids have bicycles, they can ride to school in ninety minutes. After school, they ride ninety minutes back home before going fishing for dinner. The nearest doctor is fifty miles away in an overfilled clinic.[84] On Sundays you can sleep in, meaning you get up at 5 a.m.

Whether we like it or not, we are all interdependent, and global citizenship is in, parochialism is out. Being merely a national citizen is passé. But far from a fad, being a global citizen may be necessary for our future. Take any of the mega-issues of our time: AIDS, war and the arms trade, environmental destruction, poverty, debt crises, or transnational terrorism. What do they all have in common? They all transcend national borders and cannot be solved within the realm of the nation-state. Unless we are able to transcend our national borders as well, we have no hope of dealing successfully with the world we live in.

Lab.

Observe your own global citizenship. Make it a practice to remember the common humanity of all people when you ride or drive to work, watch television, or read the news. See the cultures, the creeds, the customs. Feel the planet under your feet when you walk.

But if globalization is such a unifying force, why do we have to care about local cultures when virtually everyone in the world today drinks Coke, wears Levi's or a Swatch, and works on Windows or a Mac?

Not true, however. For one, tastes differ: teenage boys in Botswana might discuss cows with the same passion U.S. teenagers reserve for sports cars. Second, the very patterns of thought are culturally based, too. Although philosophers and psychologists have assumed for more than a century that the same basic processes underlie all human thought—a penchant for rationality, categorization, and linear thinking in terms of cause and effect—they are now finding that the very patterns of thinking vary from culture to culture because they are culturally constructed. "We used to think that everybody uses categories in the same way, that logic plays the same kind of role for everyone in the understanding of everyday life, that memory, perception, rule application and so on are the same," said Richard Nisbett, a social psychologist at the University of Michigan. He and his colleagues found that people not only think about different things; they think differently. "We're now arguing that cognitive processes are just far more malleable than mainstream psychology assumed." Dr. Nisbett's study, conducted in the United States, Japan, China, and Korea, found that Easterners appear to think more "holistically," to pay more attention to context and relationships, rely more on experience than on abstract logic, and show more tolerance for contradiction.

For example, asked to analyze a conflict between mothers and daughters, American test subjects quickly sided with one or the other, while Chinese subjects tended to see merit on both sides, commenting for example that "Both the mothers and the daughters have failed to understand each other."

In one study, students from Japan and the United States were asked to comment on an animated underwater scene in which one large fish swam among smaller fish and other aquatic life. Japanese subjects made 70 percent more statements about the background environment than did Americans, and twice as many statements about the relationships between animate and inanimate objects. "Americans were much more likely to zero in on the biggest fish, the brightest object, the fish moving the fastest," Dr. Nisbett said. "That's where the money is as far as they are concerned."

A small word like "yes" can have different meanings. Westerners might say "yes" to the action or request, while Asians might say "yes" to the context of the relationship. They both mean "yes," but in vastly different contexts. Insigniam founding partner Shideh Bina wrote this message to a contact in Shanghai in September 2011: "Yes, I can be in Shanghai on Oct 21. Early in the day would be best and I am flexible. Please let me know as soon as you have a confirm so I can change my flights. By the way, do you know P.E.? Is it useful if we indicate to him that we will be having this meeting? I think it might be effective for David to know we have this relationship. You are the expert on this dynamic—let me know what you think. Shideh"

The contact wrote back: "How long should we request for the meeting? Let me know your flexibility for that day. I will work with (Mr. X's) office to book the time.

"In a meeting, hence short writing . . . Dr. A.B."

One of her business partners who had worked extensively in Asia told Shideh that the context behind Dr. A.B.'s response was Chinese for "Don't contact him." Her contact had said "No" in a very contextual and holistic way. Or rather, the contact had said "Yes," but only to the relationship, not to the meeting. The bottom line is, culture matters, regardless of globalization.

Note, however, that cultural differences are not written into the genes. For example, many Asian-Americans born in the United States are indistinguishable in their thought patterns from European-Americans. But if history is an indicator, fundamental cultural differences will stay around for a long time. Western thinking has existed at least since ancient Greece, favoring adversarial debate, logical argument and analytic deduction. In the East, meanwhile, an appreciation for complexity, context, and the "yin and yang" of life has been cultivated for many centuries.[85]

Lab.

One benefit of globalization is that you can get many periodicals online (on www.ceoexpress.com/default.asp for instance). Select your periodicals and make it a practice to read them regularly to maintain and upgrade your world knowledge. For example, *The Week* gives a digest of news on current topics from media outlets in multiple cultures.

Go back to your key objective from the end of chapter 1. Go to Wikipedia and look up one country you want to understand.

Be a global citizen in all your actions and all your thinking. Live as though each of your actions had an impact somewhere on the planet—they probably do. We are interconnected, and our connections are only increasing.

What is Your Cross-Cultural IQ?

Before we go to the next chapter, I would like you to do a quick multiple choice exercise. (Sorry, but exercises are good for you.) It is called "What Is Your Cross-Cultural IQ?" Check the right answer for each statement:

A. Generally, Swiss business people, relative to Americans, prefer:
   1. Thicker, more detailed legal contracts.
   2. Thinner, less detailed legal contracts.
   3. Contracts with the same level of detail.

B. George Tailor works as a supervisor for an engineering company in Riyadh, Saudi Arabia. Back in the UK he had a reputation for speaking his mind and by doing so getting the best out of his staff. At the current project in Riyadh, he supervises twelve British and nearly fifty Saudi staff. After a few months George has become increasingly frustrated by what he sees as a less than effective Saudi team. Their lack of competence and slow work pace is worrying George. What should he do to bring the Saudi staff back into line?
   1. Publicly reprimand a few of the Saudi staff to ensure the message gets across to them all. By doing so he will also establish who is boss.
   2. Pick one member of the Saudi staff to explain his worries to. This staff member will then be used to relay George's opinions to the rest.
   3. Speak to as many members of staff individually or in small groups, explaining his viewpoint and encouraging them to better their work practice and enthusiasm.
   4. Report them to his manager, a Saudi national, and let him deal with them.

C A Singaporean colleague invites you to his home for dinner. It is appropriate to:
   1. Bring wine.
   2. Bring baked goods or fruit for the whole family.
   3. Bring four flowers.

D There are three of you interviewing an Afghani man for a position in your company. Of the interviewers, two of you are women. The interviewee only ever gives eye contact to the man and never to the women. This is because:

1. He is nervous around women.
2. He is showing respect.
3. He sees women as second class citizens.

E. In meetings, Germans generally prefer, compared to Americans:
   1. A more structured agenda.
   2. A less structured agenda.
   3. The same level of structure.

F. You are the new manager in an Indian office. You ask one of your supervisors to move a desk and place it in another corner of the office. The next day you notice it has not yet been done. Why?
   1. The supervisor was offended you asked him/her and refused to do anything about it.
   2. The supervisor could not find a laborer to move it and would not do so him- or herself.
   3. Things get done slowly in India.

G. Eastern Europeans, in general, compared to Western Europeans, show:
   1. More leadership and initiative.
   2. Less leadership and initiative.
   3. About the same level of leadership and initiative.

H. Bob de Jonge and his Thai associate, Chaiwat Soonvichai, are walking into a meeting in Bangkok. Chaiwat asks Bob casually, "Do you have the latest marketing portfolio with you?" Bob stops in his tracks and slaps his forehead. "Why on earth didn't you ask me that earlier? Now there's no time to go back and get it." The two continue on and conduct a successful meeting. A month later, Chaiwat leaves the company. What went wrong?
   1. Chaiwat saw the slapping of the forehead as an insult to his intelligence.
   2. Chaiwat felt a great loss of face through Bob's reaction

and felt compelled to leave the company.

3. Bob should have apologized to Chaiwat after the meeting as the missing portfolio had no negative effect.

4. Bob's reaction was seen as hot-headed and Chaiwat construed that as a bad sign in terms of an employer.

I. Compared to American business people, Japanese business people:

1. Take longer to build consensus because they give each team member a chance to comment.

2. Take less time to build consensus because leaders impose their views.

3. Take about the same time to build consensus because both 1. and 2. are true.

J. When greeting a Muslim woman, which of these should you do?

1. Wait for her to extend a hand before shaking hands.

2. Shake hands to avoid the possibility of causing offense.

3. Not greet her as this will cause her to lose face.

K. Americans are seen by other cultures to be mainly:

1. Individualist and moralist.

2. Capitalist and short-term oriented.

3. Both 1 and 2.

L. A Brazilian makes an "O" with his thumb and forefinger. This means:

1. A four-letter word.

2. Everything ok.

3. Something very small.

How did you do? If you had nine to twelve correct answers, very good! If fewer than nine answers were correct, you may want to make a systematic effort to develop your global citizenship. (For a quiz focusing on a target culture, see http://www.kwintessential .co.uk/resources/culture-tests.html)

[Correct answers: A2; B3; C2; D2; E1; F2; G2; H3; I3; J1; K3; L2]

Chapter Five

How to Avoid Culture Clashes

We aren't passengers on Spaceship Earth, we're the crew.
We aren't residents on this planet, we're citizens.
The difference in both cases is responsibility.

Rusty Schweikert, astronaut

Now that you have assessed your cross-cultural knowledge, let's see how we can bridge cultural differences. Here is an example of a paragon of cultural integration, the EU:

The European Commission announced that an agreement had been reached to adopt English as the preferred language for European communications, rather than German, which was the other possibility.[86]

As part of the negotiations, the British government conceded that English spelling had some room for improvement and accepted a five-year phased plan for what will be known as EuroEnglish (Euro for short).

In the first year, "s" will be used instead of the soft "c." Sertainly, sivil servants will resieve this news with joy. Also, the hard "c" will be replaced with "k." Not only will this klear up konfusion, but typewriters kan have one less letter.

There will be growing publik enthusiasm in the sekond year, then the troublesome "ph" will be replaced by "f." This will make words like "fotograf" 20 persent shorter.

In the third year, publik akseptanse of the new spelling kan be expekted to reach the stage where more komplikated changes are possible. Govemments will enkorage the removal of double letters, which have always ben a deterent to akurate speling. Also, al wil agre that the horible mes of silent "e"s in the languag is disgrasful, and they would go.

By the fourth year, peopl wil be reseptiv to steps such as replasing "th" by "z" and "W" by "V."

During ze fifz year, ze unesesary "o" kan be dropd from vords kontaining "ou," and similar changes vud of kors be aplid to ozer kombinations of leters. After zis fifz yer, ve vil hav a reli sensibl riten styl. Zer vil be no mor trubls or difikultis and evrivun vil find it ezi tu understand ech ozer. Ze drem vil finali kum tru.

Given that the German chancellor has been wielding the powers of a de facto European president of late, who knows when this tongue-in-cheek possibility will become reality?

Seriously, there are solutions for culture clash. Danone SA reduced its failure rate among expat managers from 35 to 3 percent in the three years since it started using a relocation assessment program. Motorola learned from its early Iridium mistakes, too: the company now uses a workplace simulation program to identify and evaluate its international managers. General Electric used to be an American company working internationally, treating the world outside the United States simply as an export market. But that is changing: the day is not far off when GE will earn more outside the United States than domestically. GE needs to build global skills. Jack Welch, the former chairman and CEO of General Electric and one of the most revered business leaders of our time, recognized this several years before his retirement in a speech to GE executives:

> The Jack Welch of the future cannot be like me. I spent my entire career in the United States. The next head of General Electric will be somebody who spent time in Bombay, in Hong Kong, in Buenos Aires. We have to send our best and greatest overseas and make sure they have the training that

will allow them to be the global leaders who will make G.E. flourish in the future.

Welch's successor, Jeffrey Immelt, has continued backing these words with action. New hires at GE's Crotonville training center are given crash courses in global issues (disclosure: my colleagues and I gave some of these). Senior executives are routinely sent on four-week trips to foreign markets, upon which they return to Crotonville to brief top executives. GE's team in China engages employees, suppliers, and customers at the leadership development center in its Asia headquarters. In Europe, the company delivers leadership courses to its executives from across the continent at its global research center just outside of Munich and its international headquarters in Brussels. GE partnered with the Mubadala Development Company in Abu Dhabi to host a corporate learning program for GE leaders. In 2008, GE took more than 280 people across eighteen GE businesses on an Asia tour to Shanghai, New Delhi, and Dubai. That same year, a class of fifty top-level GE executives traveled to Nigeria, Mozambique, and Kenya to explore growth opportunities and understand the challenges of the African continent. Participants held audiences with government, business, and academic leaders to discuss where GE could provide long-term, sustainable solutions. The intention of all this is to build what Welch used to call a "multipolar and multicultural company."

But on an individual level, how do you build multicultural skills? This and the next chapters suggest several tools: Do's and Taboos, Lawrence of Arabia's *Twenty-Seven Articles,* and what I call the Global Integrator™ and the Global Leader Pyramid™.

Tool 1: Do's and Taboos of Global Citizenship

The first tool is a set of guidelines for global citizens. These guidelines sensitize you and your colleagues to fourteen Do's and Taboos, the unwritten rules of conduct when working across cultures.

Watch your hosts and do what they do. For example, American-style sporting analogies ("slam dunk," "cover all bases," or "step up to the plate") will unlikely be understood or buy you any points. Americans ought to remember that what most others call "football" is what they call "soccer." If that is just the start, their best bet is to steer clear of sports analogies altogether.

Never take English for granted. Remember that if English is not your hosts' first language, they have to make it work for you with every English sentence they speak—or hear. When Insigniam consultants came to genuinely appreciate the underlying arrogance of going to another person's country and require them to speak English, the firm's global business sky-rocketed. When going to another country, it might not be a bad idea to start by apologizing for not speaking their language (though the apology works only if the intent is authentic). Or at the very least, to ask for whom English is not their mother tongue, and to acknowledge the effort it takes your hosts to listen and speak in another language and to constantly translate what is said in their heads.

Respect people, their ideas, and their cultures. Be polite, on your best behavior, not loud—after all, you are a guest. Never make a face, grimace or worse yet, exclaim anything close to "gross!" at foods you see others eat. At the same time, expect that at some point your boundaries will be violated—and be prepared to stay calm and gracious. In certain Middle Eastern countries, for example, it is perfectly acceptable to ask how much your home or car cost, and to openly discuss price tags Americans usually keep private.

Interact with people as individuals, not as a culture. Resist the urge to generalize. At its extreme, generalization borders on racism.

Listen when people tell you all their issues, especially at the beginning of your visit. Listening is a vastly underrated skill. Resist the urge to immediately resolve the issues—simply hearing them might be enough to dissolve them.

Be open to input and to learning. You can learn enormous-
ly from other cultures (about them *and* yourself—when I lived in
India and Japan, I learned about those cultures, but perhaps
more importantly, I revealed my own blind spots and hidden
values, both Swiss and American in my case). If you feel that
you know a culture already, that there is nothing new, you will
be right: there will indeed be nothing to learn. Assume that you
don't know.

Remember that understanding even one country or culture
can be a quest of a lifetime. It is not something you can tick off
on a checklist and be done with.

If you don't know, say so. Don't wing it. Ask, and people
will support you. At their core, humans are happy to help.

Find the gate to the village if it is fenced in. Do your
research, watch, and observe. Do *not* take the village by storm.
Force rarely works and should be used as a last resort and only
when all other options have been exhausted.

Talk to someone who is clear whenever you are not clear.
Keep a shared understanding on your mission with your partners
back home. For example, check in on a weekly basis with your
superior or partner at headquarters—somebody who can help
you step back from the challenges and make sense of them.

Remember that your advice is noise in their ears,
unless they ask for it.

Follow up on promises and agreements. "I heard you say
the package would be here by 3 p.m. and it is not. This comes as
a surprise." Do not accuse, do not get upset, but do inquire until
you are satisfied.

Roll with the punches if you are sabotaged. Free yourself
from the attachment to a particular picture or form. There may
be another pathway to your goal than the one you had in mind.

Know that you *will* make mistakes; the question is how
to recover. (Already the ancient Chinese sage Confucius is
reported to have said that "the greatest glory in living lies not in
never falling, but in rising every time we fall.")

And don't forget the most important thing: one kiss in the United States, two in Britain and most of Europe, three in Switzerland and Holland . . .

Above all, do your homework. Before you go to any culture other than your own, research enough about the target culture, the language, and the history so that you can stand in their shoes and see the world from their point of view. With resources like Wikipedia and Wikitravel available on the Internet, this is no longer a costly or time-consuming burden. When I went to Kazakhstan to work with the Kazakh prime minister and his cabinet of ministers, I realized that I knew next to nothing about the Kazakh culture. So I took a few hours to poke around on Wikitravel and Wikipedia and learn about the culture.

The investment paid off handsomely. After I was introduced as the workshop leader, I said a few words in Kazakh. It was simply an apology: "Ladies and gentlemen, I am sorry that I don't speak Kazakh. Thank you for listening through a translator." I got a standing ovation! Then, once the workshop had begun, I noticed that the cabinet ministers were reluctant to participate. No wonder: the prime minister was sitting literally three meters from me. Knowing the history of Kazahkstan as a Soviet republic for much of the twentieth century, I sensed that they were afraid of saying something wrong or stupid and being penalized for that. So I used a factoid I had picked up in my preparation and said: "Ladies and gentlemen, may I remind you that the original meaning of 'Kazakh' is 'free citizen', or 'free spirit.' So I encourage you to live up to that meaning and express your thoughts fully." They laughed and applauded, and I could see that they felt I understood their culture. From then on, they (well, most of them, a critical mass) interacted more freely.

Tool 2: Lawrence of Arabia — Quintessential Global Citizen

The second tool is what I consider a useful guideline for dealing effectively with a target culture: *The Twenty-Seven Articles* by T. E. Lawrence, commonly known as "Lawrence of Arabia."[87] Although he wrote them specifically for British officers stationed in Arab countries and claims below that they are "of course not suitable" in any other context, I beg to differ with the legendary Lawrence. I have found his *Articles* relevant anywhere and quote the essay at length:

> The following notes have been expressed in commandment form for greater clarity and to save words. They are however only my personal conclusions, arrived at gradually while I worked in the Hedjaz and now put on paper as stalking horses for beginners in the Arab armies . . . They are of course not suitable to any other person's need, or applicable unchanged in any particular situation. Handling Hedjaz Arabs is an art, not a science, with exceptions and no obvious rules . . .
>
> 1. Go easy just for the first few weeks. A bad start is difficult to atone for, and the Arabs form their judgments on externals that we ignore. When you have reached the inner circle in a tribe you can do as you please with yourself and them.
>
> 2. Learn all you can about your Ashraf and Bedu. Get to know their families, clans and tribes, friends and enemies, wells, hills and roads. Do all this by listening and by indirect inquiry. Do not ask questions. Get to speak their dialect of Arabic, not yours. Until you can understand their allusions avoid getting deep into conversation, or you will drop bricks. Be a little stiff at first.
>
> 3. In matters of business deal only with the commander of the Army, column, or party in which you serve. Never give orders to anyone at all, and reserve your directions or advice for the C.O., however great the temptation (for efficiency's sake) of dealing direct with his underlings. Your place is advisory, and your advice is due to the commander alone. Let him see that this is your conception of your duty, and that his is to be the sole executive of your joint plans.

4. Win and keep the confidence of your leader. Strengthen his prestige at your expense before others when you can. Never refuse or quash schemes he may put forward: but ensure that they are put forward in the first instance privately to you. Always approve them, and after praise modify them insensibly, causing the suggestions to come from him, until they are in accord with your own opinion. When you attain this point, hold him to it, keep a tight grip of his ideas, and push him forward as firmly as possible, but secretly so that no one but himself (and he not too clearly) is aware of your pressure.

5. Remain in touch with your leader as constantly and unobtrusively as you can. Live with him, that at meal times and at audiences you may be naturally with him in his tent. Formal visits to give advice are not so good as the constant dropping of ideas in casual talk. When stronger sheikhs come in for the first time to swear allegiance and offer services, clear out of the tent. If their first impression is of foreigners in the confidence of the Sherif, it will do the Arab cause much harm. (. . .)

8. Your ideal position is when you are present and not noticed. Do not be too intimate, too prominent, or too earnest. Avoid being identified too long or too often with any tribal sheikh, even if C.O. (Commanding Officer, ed.) of the expedition. To do your work you must be above jealousies, and you lose prestige if you are associated with a tribe or clan, and its inevitable feuds. Sherifs are above all blood-feuds and local rivalries, and form the only principle of unity among the Arabs. Let your name, therefore, be coupled always with a Sherif's, and share his attitude towards the tribe. When the moment comes for action put yourself publicly under his orders. The Bedu will then follow suit. (. . .)

11. The foreigner and Christian is not a popular person in Arabia. However friendly and informal the treatment of yourself may be, remember always that your foundations are very sandy ones. Wave a Sherif in front of you

like a banner, and hide your own mind and person. If you succeed you will have hundreds of miles of country and thousands of men under your orders, and for this it is worth bartering the outward show.

12. Cling tight to your sense of humor. You will need it every day. A dry irony is the most useful type, and repartee of a personal and not too broad character will double your influence with the Chiefs. Reproof if wrapped up in some smiling form will carry further and last longer than the most violent speech. The power of mimicry or parody is valuable but use it sparingly for it is more dignified than humor. Do not cause a laugh at a Sherif except amongst Sherifs.

13. Never lay hands on an Arab—you degrade yourself. You may think the resultant obvious increase of outward respect a gain to you: but what you have really done is to build a wall between you and their inner selves. It is difficult to keep quiet when everything is being done wrong, but the less you lose your temper the greater your advantage. Also then you will not go mad yourself.

14. While very difficult to drive, the Bedu are easy to lead, if you have the patience to bear with them. The less apparent your interferences the more you influence. They are willing to follow your advice and do what you wish, but they do not mean you or anyone else to be aware of that. It is only after the end of all annoyances that you find at bottom their real fund of good will.

15. Do not try to do too much with your own hands. Better the Arabs do it tolerably than that you do it perfectly. It is their war, and you are to help them, not to win it for them. Actually also under the very odd conditions of Arabia, your practical work will not be as good as perhaps you think it is.

16. If you can, without being too lavish, forestall presents to yourself. A well placed gift is often most effective in winning over a suspicious Sheikh. Never receive a present without giving a liberal return, but you may

delay this return (while letting its ultimate certainty be known) if you require a particular service from the giver. Do not let them ask you for things, since their greed will then make them look upon you only as a cow to milk. (. . .)

18. Disguise is not advisable. Except in special areas let it be clearly known that you are a British officer and a Christian. At the same time if you can wear Arab kit when with the tribes you will acquire their trust and intimacy to a degree impossible in uniform. It is however dangerous and difficult. They make no special allowances for you when you dress like them. Breaches of etiquette not charged against a foreigner are not condoned to you in Arab clothes. You will be like an actor in a foreign theatre, playing a part day and night for months, without rest, and for an anxious stake. Complete success, which is when the Arabs forget your strangeness and speak naturally before you, counting you one of themselves, is perhaps only attainable in character: while half success (all that most of us will strive for—the other costs too much) is easier to win in British things, and you yourself will last longer, physically and mentally, in the comfort that they mean. Also then the Turks will not hang you, when you're caught. (. . .)

20. If you wear Arab things at all, go the whole way. Leave your English friends and customs on the coast, and fall back on Arab habits entirely. It is possible, starting thus to level with them, for the Europeans to beat the Arabs at their own game, for we had stronger motives for our action, and put more heart into it than they. If you can surpass them, you have taken an immense stride toward complete success, but the strain of living and thinking in a foreign and half-understood language, the savage food, strange clothes, and still stranger ways, with the complete loss of privacy and quiet, and the impossibility of ever realizing your watchful imitation of the others for months

on end, provide such an added stress to the ordinary difficulties of dealing with the Bedu, the climate, and the Turks, that this road should not be chosen without serious thought.

[This is one rule where I disagree with Lawrence. In my experience, dressing exactly like our hosts is neither necessary nor effective. You cannot hope to ever bow exactly like a Japanese businessman, and not bowing perfectly has to my knowledge never been a deal-breaker in international business.]

21. Religious discussions will be fairly frequent. Say what you like about your own side, and avoid criticism of theirs, unless you know that the point is external, when you may score heavily by proving it so. With the Bedu Islam is so all-pervading an element that there is with religiosity, little fervour, and no regard for externals. Do not think from their conduct that they are careless. Their conviction of the truth of their faith, and its share in every act and thought and principle of their daily life is so intimate and intense as to be unconscious, unless roused by opposition. Their religion is as much a part of nature to them as is sleep, or food.

22. Do not try to trade on what you know of fighting. The Hedjaz confounds ordinary tactics. Learn the Bedu principles of war as thoroughly and as quickly as you can, for till you know them your advice will be no good to the Sherif. Unnumbered generations of tribal raids have taught them more about some parts of the business than we will ever know. In familiar conditions they fight well, but strange events cause panic. Keep your unit small. Their raiding parties are usually from one hundred to two hundred men, and if you take a crowd they only get confused. Also their sheikhs, while admirable company commandoes, are too set to learn to handle the equivalents of battalions or regiments. Don't attempt unusual things, unless they appeal to the sporting instinct Bedu have so strongly, or unless success is obvious. If the

objective is a good one (booty) they will attack like fiends: they are splendid scouts, their mobility gives you the advantage that will win their local war, they make proper use of their knowledge of the country (don't take tribesmen to places they do not know), and the gazelle-hunters, who form a proportion of the better men, are great shots at visible targets. A Sheikh from one tribe cannot give orders to men from another: a Sherif is necessary to command a mixed tribal force. If there is plunder in prospect, and the odds are at all equal, you will win. Do not waste Bedu attacking trenches (they will not stand casualties) or in trying to defend a position, for they cannot sit still without slacking. The more unorthodox and Arab your proceedings the more likely you are to have the Turks cold, for they lack initiative and expect you to. Don't play for safety.

23. The open reason that Bedu give you for action or inaction may be true, but always there will be better reasons left for you to divine. You must find these inner reasons (they will be denied, but are none the less in operation) before shaping your arguments for one course or others. Allusion is more effective than logical exposition: they dislike concise expression. Their minds work just as ours do, but on different premises. There is nothing unreasonable, incomprehensible, or inscrutable in the Arab. Experience of them, and knowledge of their prejudices will enable you to foresee their attitude and possible course of action in nearly every case.

24. Do not mix Bedu and Syrians, or trained men and tribesmen. You will get work out of neither, for they hate each other. I have never seen a successful combined operation, but many failures. In particular, ex-officers of the Turkish army however Arab in feeling and blood and language, are hopeless with Bedu. They are narrowminded in tactics, unable to adjust themselves to irregular warfare, clumsy in Arab etiquette, swollen-headed to the extent of being incapable of politeness to a

tribesman for more than a few minutes, impatient, and usually helpless on the road, in action. Your orders (if you were unwise enough to give any) would be more readily obeyed by Bedouins than those of any Mohammedan Syrian officer. Arab townsmen and Arab tribesmen regard each other mutually as poor relations—and poor relations are much more objectionable than poor strangers.

25. In spite of ordinary Arab example avoid too free talk about women. It is as difficult a subject as religion, and their standards are so unlike our own, that a remark harmless in English may appear as unrestrained to them, as some of their statements would look to us, if translated literally. (. . .)

27. The beginning and ending of the secret of handling Arabs is unremitting study of them. Keep always on your guard; never say an inconsidered thing, or do an unnecessary thing; watch yourself and your companions all the time; hear all that passes, search out what is going on beneath the surface, read their characters, discover their tastes and their weaknesses, and keep everything you find out to yourself. Bury yourself in Arab circles, have no interests and no ideas except the work in hand, so that your brain shall he saturated with one thing only, and you realize your part deeply enough to avoid the little slips that would undo the work of weeks. Your success will be just proportioned to the amount of mental effort you devote to it.

True, Lawrence represents an empire that subjugated not only the Raj, but also many other peoples in what it called a Commonwealth, which was often repressive. We cannot forget the massacre in India where British troops slaughtered thousands of Indians for fear of India's movement for independence. Nevertheless, Lawrence has something to say that is more pertinent than ever. His final guideline, to "Keep always on your guard; never say an inconsidered thing, or do an unnecessary thing; watch yourself and your companions all the time; hear all that passes, search out what is going on beneath the surface, read their characters, discover their tastes and their weaknesses" rings true for anyone doing business not only with Islamic cultures but with any value-system not your own.

Chapter Six

Tools for Decoding Any Culture (Not Least, Your Own)

Spanish is the language for lovers, Italian for singers, French for diplomats, German for horses, and English for geese.
H.L. Mencken

Near the other end of the continuum from Lawrence of Arabia's insightful operating principles are the usually well-meant and always hilarious messages in this sampling of English signs from around the world:[88]

- On the menu of a Swiss restaurant: "Our wines leave you nothing to hope for."
- In a Belgrade hotel elevator: "Please leave your values at the front desk."
- In a Japanese hotel: "You are invited to take advantage of the chambermaid."
- In an Austrian hotel catering to skiers: "Not to perambulate the corridors in the hours of repose in the boots of ascension."
- Alongside a Hong Kong tailor shop: "Ladies may have a fit upstairs."
- At a Rhodes tailor shop: "Order your summer suit. Because is big rush, we will execute customers in strict rotation."
- In a Zurich hotel: "Because of the impropriety of entertaining guests of the opposite sex in the bedroom, it is suggested that the lobby be used for this purpose."
- In a Norwegian cocktail lounge: "Ladies are requested not to have children in the bar."
- At an Acapulco hotel: "The manager has personally passed all the water served here."

- In a Japanese information booklet about using a hotel air conditioner: "Cooles and Heates: If you want just condition of warm in your room, please control yourself."

On a more serious note, and going a level deeper than the rather generic ground rules of the previous chapter, the next few pages help you decipher quickly any culture, including your own—which can be the trickiest challenge in cross-cultural management. As I said in the previous chapter, when I lived in India, I learned a lot about the prevailing mindset in India; but the real eye-openers were about my own Swiss culture, meaning my unexamined assumptions that ranged from punctuality to detail-orientation to neutrality. This chapter offers two tools designed to assist you in quickly decoding the cultural preferences (your own as well as the target culture's) so that your actions will be along the appropriate cultural pathways: what some have called the Onion Model of Culture[89] and another tool of eight cultural dimensions that I call the Global Integrator™.

Tool 3: Decoding Culture: From the Obvious to the Hidden

This tool trains your muscle for decoding any cultural mindset, be it of a country or a corporation. You can distinguish three layers of culture. The outer and most apparent layer is made up of the visible and audible signs and behaviors you can readily observe: logos, dress codes, styles, architecture, movies, music, how people eat or how they talk, for example. The middle layer is how people justify and rationalize the outer layer: "The way we do things around here is . . . because . . ." The third and innermost layer is what is truly culture: the past decisions that have become so automatic as to become invisible, automatic, even unconscious. What is it that people don't even know they don't know? That is culture.

Now, how do you decode this innermost, invisible culture? An elegant way involves four facets. The first is to understand the ideology and values of the *founders*. The myth of William Tell, who ambushed the Hapsburg vassal Gessler and catalyzed a move-ment to throw out the Hapsburgs and the *Rütlischwur,* the solemn oath by a group of farmers from the center of Switzerland who founded Switzerland in 1291, are telling if we want to understand why Switzerland jealously guards its neutrality, why it joined the United Nations only in 2002, and why it adamantly refuses to join the European Union today. Moving across the Atlantic, Thomas Jefferson and the other founders of the United States enshrined their values of life, liberty, and the pursuit of happiness, still underpinnings of U.S. culture today. By contrast, no European constitution contains such a fundamental right to pursue happi-ness. The Swiss Constitution, for example, limits freedom with responsibility: ". . .conscious of our common achievements and our responsibility towards future generations, certain that free is only who uses his freedom, and that the strength of a people is measured by the welfare of the weak . . ."[90]

To understand Israel, you would want to learn about David Ben-Gurion, a founder and the first prime minister; learning about him would tell you a lot about Israel's core values. Ben-Gurion was once upbraided by Israel's President Chaim Weizmann for appearing at a formal dinner in the typical fashion of Israel's pio-neers, with an unbuttoned collar and no jacket or tie. "How can you show up dressed like this at a state dinner?" Weizmann asked. "Think of all the foreign guests who are here." "But Winston Churchill," Ben-Gurion claimed, "gave me his permis-sion." "What do you mean Winston Churchill gave you permis-sion?" Weizmann asked. "He's not even here!" "Well," Ben-Gurion explained with a smile, "When I last visited London, Churchill said to me, 'Mr. Prime Minister, in Israel you may dress that way, but not in London'!" This little vignette tells you not only about Ben-Gurion's sense of humor, but also about the Israeli culture's defi-ance, its bucking of international norms, and its informal style.

A second access to the invisible culture are its *heroes.* Australia is often, and only half-jokingly, called a "nation of con-victs" because the British Empire filled its penal colonies there with rebels and criminals, some of whom went on to found the nation in addition to some of its core values, including fairness and beating the system. One of Australia's greatest heroes is Ned Kelly, one of its most wanted men in the late nineteenth century. Ned and his brother Dan were at large in the Australian bush after killing three police officers; at one point the government reward for their capture rose to an astonishing 8,000 pounds (some $2 million today). Finally, in a legendary battle with police, Ned received 28 bullet wounds to his arms, legs, feet, groin, and hands—but survived, only to be sentenced to death and hanged at the age of 25 in Melbourne, despite protests by thousands of supporters. To this day Ned Kelly lives on as an admired, if infamous, hero who stood up to authority.

To take a modern-day hero (and quite the opposite of Ned Kelly), the Swiss tennis pro Roger Federer epitomizes Swiss core values like being nice, diplomacy, neutrality, hard work, discipline, and quality.

A third access to decoding a culture is to see who are the *outcasts*—in other words, what behaviors are not permissible, even taboo, in the dominant culture. For example, when I was in Cuba, I saw how the Latin machismo culture, including the state, oppresses and ridicules homosexuals. In the U.S. culture, atheism is permissible, but atheists find themselves clearly outside the mainstream, which is suspicious of non-believers. It is virtually impossible for atheists to win political office; the only openly atheist member of the U.S. Congress is Pete Stark of California; the only atheist at state level is Ernie Chambers of Nebraska; and when the Secular Coalition of America tried to find how many atheists were among the 500,000 or so elected officials at all levels, it found five.[91]

The third step is to look through the history of a culture and identify wars and other (for instance economic) crises that are often *defining moments* in shaping a culture. The first and second world wars helped shape the self-understanding in U.S. culture that America is the good guy fighting against the bad guys and saving the world. President Woodrow Wilson declared that the United States was fighting World War I to "make the world safe for democracy." By entering World War II, the U.S. prevented Nazi Germany's world dominance. Both wars ended the Monroe Doctrine, which had mandated that America stay out of meddling in European affairs. But by 1944, the Roosevelt administration had actively espoused a new role—saving the world. From then on, the United States saw itself as a benevolent hegemon, ridding the world of Nazism, then Communism, and most recently from terrorism. Subsequent U.S. administrations imposed democracy in Germany and Japan, underwrote much of the UN system, went to war in Korea and Vietnam (and more recently in the Persian Gulf and Afghanistan), monitored elections in Zambia, and so forth. "We know what is good for the world" had become an unquestioned assumption not only in U.S. foreign policy, but also in many U.S. multinational corporations.

These four facets—founders, heroes, villains, and defining moments—are key to decoding any culture. In addition, there are other aspects that can give you access to revealing the mindset. Particularly, before you do business in another country, here are several key areas you will want to understand, ideally before you hit the ground:

Economy. Find the engines of the country's or region's economy. What are its most important sectors? How dependent is the economy on outside resources and trade? International trade accounts for under 20 percent of the GDP of the United States and Japan, compared to over half the GDP of smaller OECD countries, namely Austria, Belgium, the Czech Republic, Denmark, Hungary, Ireland, Korea, Luxembourg, the Netherlands, the Slovak Republic, Sweden, and Switzerland.[92] Greater dependence on external trade tends to make a country much more open to other cultures.

History. Identify key formative events, factors, and actors in the culture's history and economic development (historic leaders, wars, revolutions, and economic crises). Identify the importance of foreign influences. For instance, to understand Switzerland, you would have to appreciate that it has safeguarded its neutrality since 1815, has not had a war since 1848, and had its last general strike in 1919. These events have helped shape the Swiss culture's aversion to conflict, for example.

Geography. Look at a map of the country. Is it locked in by natural borders or exposed? What are its immediate neighbors? What are its natural resources? Japan and Britain are island nations, which may have contributed to their aloofness from their respective continents (the United Kingdom being reluctant to join the Eurozone, Japan having kept itself insulated for much of its history).

Religion. What is the country's dominant religion? What core values does that religion prescribe and what behaviors does it proscribe? What, according to the dominant religion, are the obligations of the individual and the community? Catholicism in France and Italy provides absolution from sins and in so doing might encourage a certain joie de vivre (although some of my French and Italian friends might disagree).

Government. If the country is governed by a constitution, read it (most national constitutions are posted on the Web). What is the authority of government institutions, political parties, and regulatory agencies? What role does government play vis-à-vis companies, trade and foreign influence? For example, the United States has a strong antitrust culture and a belief in the value of competition, while most European countries long believed in cartels as a tool of economic statecraft, and have come to espouse anti-cartel laws only recently.

Outsiders. Are there many immigrants in the culture? Is the country open to them or closed? Who is seen as going against the grain of the dominant culture? For example, although some have called Barack Obama a "Commie," the fact is that since 1924, Communist candidates for the U.S. presidency have never won more than 0.26 percent of the vote; and to see whether smokers are insiders or outsiders in U.S. culture, just do the experiment and light up in public.

Media. Who in the country has access to world media like CNN or BBC? How many people have access to the Internet? In Kenya, a small elite in government and academia accesses the

Web, while many in the general population depend on the radio for news and weather forecasts. Which media are the most widely circulated? Americans watch TV the most, while Russians and Germans have the highest newspaper readership.

Education. Determine the country's literacy rate and the value and mode of learning and training. How important is educational background for credibility in business? In France, most members of the business elite have been groomed for leadership in the *Grandes Ecoles* (Great Schools). In the U.S., you can be a revered entrepreneur without as much as a college degree; Bill Gates stayed at Harvard College for only two years and Steve Jobs, Michael Dell, and Mark Zuckerberg are all college dropouts.

Mobility. How mobile are people, both up (or as the case may be, down) and laterally? In the United States, mobility is very high, people tend to be willing to move, more often to move up, while in Switzerland people tend to stay in their hometown all their lives and stay loyal to the same employer. (My father worked for Sandoz—later Novartis—for thirty-five years and stayed in Basel his entire professional life.)

Population. Find out the size of the population and the demographics. Is there a large and strong middle class? How many people live below the subsistence minimum? Who are the elite? In most sub-Saharan African countries there is barely a middle class. In Germany, the elites are members of the church, the written word, and academia, so clergy members, journalists or writers, and intellectuals have disproportionate power to shape public opinion, whereas in the United States business people, broadcast media, and Hollywood celebrities tend to have much more power and status. (Arnold Schwarzenegger's ascent from bodybuilder to Terminator to "Governator" would be rather unthinkable in his native Austria; so would his eventual descent to "Sperminator.")

Language. What is the dominant language and what other languages are spoken in the country? Are minority languages accepted and encouraged by the majority? Switzerland has established four national languages, three of which are official languages in which all government business is conducted. In 1848 Switzerland decided against a prime minister and instead designed the Federal Council, a seven-member collective executive to give all languages, all regions, and all major parties a voice in governing.

Myths. What are the inspiring war stories about the nation's past? Many national cultures nurture such mythological stories that affirm or symbolize their core values. What qualities do the heroes in these myths embody for people, and how are these values reflected in day-to-day business? Russian national myths include the fifteenth-century claim after the fall of the Byzantine Empire in 1453 that "Moscow is the Third Rome" and that Russia was the rightful successor to the Christian heritage. Later, the myths of "Slavic-Orthodox unity" and "Russian-Ukrainian–Belarusian brotherhood" served to cement the Russian, and then the Soviet, nation.

In the Middle East, the War of 1948, known to Israelis as the War of Independence, which occurred when its neighbors attacked Israel immediately after it was founded by a UN-declaration, has stayed in the national imagination ever since. One of the war's heroes, Yitzchak Rabin, later became prime minister; many Israeli national leaders come from the Israel Defense Force (IDF) or from the Mossad, the secret service: Moshe Dayan, Bibi Netanyahu, Ehud Barak, and Ariel Sharon are only a few examples of the prestige the military enjoys in Israel. The stories of the successive wars Israel had to fight for its survival have fostered a dogged determination to overcome all odds, but also at times a righteousness and defensiveness. And many Israeli business people are among the most combative negotiators in the world.

The Global Integrator™: Eight Dimensions of Culture

The spider graph on the next page can help you see the gaps between your own culture and that of any target culture. Say you wish to enter a new market such as China or India, or you want to improve collaboration with an M&A or JV partner. You can map the two cultures onto each other so that the similarities and discrepancies show up quickly and clearly. I have assigned a scale of 0 to 10 to each of eight dimensions; each should be seen as a continuum. Feel free to have a specific target culture in mind as you read the descriptions of the eight dimensions that follow.

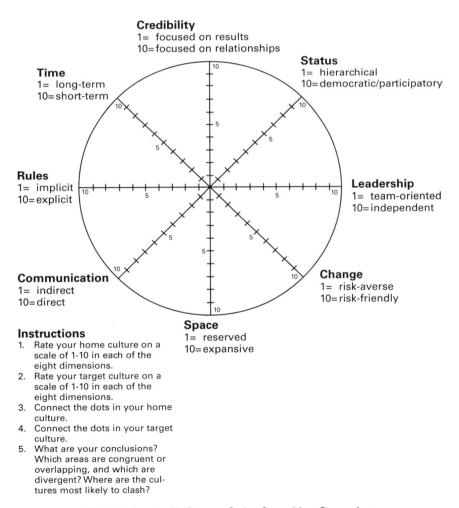

Credibility
1= focused on results
10= focused on relationships

Status
1= hierarchical
10= democratic/participatory

Time
1= long-term
10= short-term

Rules
1= implicit
10= explicit

Leadership
1= team-oriented
10= independent

Communication
1= indirect
10= direct

Change
1= risk-averse
10= risk-friendly

Space
1= reserved
10= expansive

Instructions
1. Rate your home culture on a scale of 1-10 in each of the eight dimensions.
2. Rate your target culture on a scale of 1-10 in each of the eight dimensions.
3. Connect the dots in your home culture.
4. Connect the dots in your target culture.
5. What are your conclusions? Which areas are congruent or overlapping, and which are divergent? Where are the cultures most likely to clash?

Global Integrator™. Source: Swiss Consulting Group, Inc.

Credibility (focus on results vs. focus on relationships). How do people gain or lose credibility in the culture? How measurable are results and accomplishments in people's work? How does a person's past performance influence that person's career prospects? How important are prior relationships for business? What matters more, achievements or connections? Southern European colleagues tell me that in their countries, at least as important as what you know is who you know. No matter what your track record, you can secure a top position only if you have the right connections. In the United States, by contrast, the culture is more meritocratic: your track record, not your connections, determines how far you can go. American managers put heavy emphasis on your performance. Donald Trump's results as a real estate developer spoke for themselves and qualified him, at least in the eyes of his supporters, to run for President—an unlikely scenario in Europe.

Status (hierarchical vs. democratic/participatory). Is there a steep hierarchy or is the organization flat? How is social or economic status linked to gender, race, age, or religion? What are the status and power of women in the culture? Is the style of leadership more "masculine" (hierarchical, structural) or more "feminine" (participatory, inclusive, organic)?

In the United States, managers often think nothing of bypassing their direct superior if producing the result warrants that. In fact you can score points by going directly to the top brass because that shows you are a resourceful leader. In France or Germany, the tradition of the absolutist state bureaucracy has created steep hierarchies, where bypassing your boss might be frowned upon and even seen as disloyal. In Mexico, I have seen bosses hold meetings not to interact with their teams but merely to hand out instructions. Many in the Swiss culture assume that if you or your parents are not from the elite, you probably do not deserve to lead. In the British and Australian cultures, fairness is among the most esteemed values—and their idea of fairness is to bring down or speak out against those at the top in an attempt to even the playing field.

(A British joke asks, what is the difference between an American and a British worker? Answer: the American stands at the entrance of the GM factory, sees the boss driving out in his Cadillac and says: "Goddammit, one day I'm gonna drive a Cadillac just like this!" Meanwhile, the British worker stands at the entrance of the Rolls Royce factory, sees the boss driving out in the Rolls and says: "Goddammit, one day this son of a bitch is gonna drive a bicycle just like me!")

Leadership (team-oriented vs. independent, individualism vs. collectivism, initiative vs. waiting). How are decisions made? Is individual or group decision-making preferred? Who has decision-making power, and how do people know (by rank, title, budget power, seating arrangements, treatment by or of others)? Do people show personal initiative, even unilateral action, or do they wait or ask for permission? Are employees encouraged to work together or to find solutions independently? Is individual performance praised, criticized as unilateral, or ignored altogether? Who is expected to take responsibility for breakdowns?

Leadership cultures differ from country to country, and often within countries. Many Americans have a profoundly different mindset about leadership than people from Europe or Japan do. In the United States, leadership is seen as an adventure, and people want to be leaders. In contrast, in Japan, Sweden, and Germany, the emphasis is on group consensus. A brief look at the recent history of these countries tells why some cultures might consider it dangerous to stick your neck out too much. Japanese leadership led the country to destruction and humiliation in World War II, so today Japanese companies tend to put an inordinate emphasis on consensus. For example, they hold staff meetings where everyone has to speak. I attended one that lasted two days, and the sleep I found myself fighting against was not just a result of jetlag.

In Germany, defeat in both World War I and World War II has made people very reluctant to display leadership. They want to do most things by consensus, for example through continuous cooperation between industry, labor, and government who harmonize industrial policy together instead of leaving it to chance or to the market. Although Germany is a very powerful country, many Germans shy away from overt leadership. It's no accident that Germany's chancellor is Angela Merkel, a relatively uncharismatic and consensus-oriented woman. In Sweden, two outstanding and greatly admired leaders, Dag Hammarskjöld and Olaf Palme, were both assassinated in the second half of the twentieth century. Given its already existing bias against exposing oneself by leading, the Swedish psyche may well have absorbed the lesson: being a leader is perilous. In Eastern Europe, the former Communist regimes have produced an absence of leadership, an aversion to risk, and the expectation that the state, not its citizens, should provide leadership.

Western cultures, at least in the past, have valued self-interest much more than the East did. Descartes' famous dictum "I think, therefore I am" led to a culture of individualism, self-realization, goal-achievement, but also personal property, materialism, consumption, and ultimately "me, mine and money." In Eastern cultures such as India, Japan, and China, the group matters more than it does in the West; there is a strong norm that "we do what the group says." Many people would gladly sacrifice themselves for their family, their company, or their country. This goes not only for Japan's infamous kamikaze pilots in World War II. I once asked a colleague in India if he were willing to die if that would assure the end of hunger in his country. He laughed at me and said, "But of course! What kind of question is that!"

Change (risk-averse vs. risk-friendly, continuity vs. discontinuity). Is change seen as an opportunity or a necessary evil? Are people risk-friendly or risk-averse? Are structures held as immutable or malleable? Are there sacred cows that cannot be touched? How are new ideas best presented: by letter or email, by phone or in a meeting? And by whom: a senior executive, a project team, or someone else? How mobile are people and what is the employee turnover? As we have seen, on average, Americans are much more mobile than Europeans; they move to Arizona or Florida, they change employers, they switch careers in the pursuit of opportunity, some of my former colleagues have even changed their names. Americans tend to see change as an adventure.

Space (reserved vs. expansive, close vs. distant, open vs. closed). How important is privacy, or a personalized workspace? Are work and family distinct or overlapping? What are the attitudes toward order and disorder? What is the role of nationality, status, gender, and race in building relationships? How open or closed is the economy? Is business an accepted topic at social occasions and vice versa? Are first names, last names, or titles used? People in Germany, Switzerland, or Japan tend to be more formal than they are in Brazil, Israel, or the United States. While most of my clients around the world have no problem being addressed with their first names like "Stéphanie" or "Steve," most of my German-speaking clients prefer to be addressed formally like "Mr. Brandmayr" until we have built enough trust or unless I specifically ask if we can use first names during an engagement. Japanese colleagues are addressed with their last names as "Nomura-san" or "Uekusa-san" no matter how deep the relationship.

Japan is a relatively small island with more than 125 million people, so the Japanese are careful not to use up space. When they step into an elevator, many Japanese will stand so close to the wall as to almost become one with it. They will feel invaded by you if you take up a lot of room. On the other hand, in the United States, Canada, or Australia, people are accustomed to having and using a lot of room—even the main street is called "Broadway."

Communication (indirect vs. direct, non-verbal vs. verbal, written vs. oral, self-expression vs. understanding, visceral vs.

cerebral, silence vs. talking). Are differences discussed openly or behind closed doors? What is the preferred medium to relate information—oral or written? Should people voice their opinions or should they be silent? What should you say if you don't know the answer? What is the perception of silence? How do you apologize for a mistake?

For example, people in some cultures, like in Britain or Switzerland, tend not to communicate directly but to be roundabout. An American senior executive in the U.S. audit division of a major Swiss pharmaceutical company told me she had worked for two years in the UK office and enjoyed fairly cordial relations with her British colleagues. On the eve of her departure back to the United States, a key colleague told her brusquely that he had been completely dissatisfied with her work. She asked him, "Why didn't you tell me earlier?" He thought he had conveyed his displeasure, but she had never noticed. In general, British managers won't talk straight, at least compared to American and Dutch managers, many of whom love straight talk and get right to the point.

One facet of the communication dimension is self-expression vs. understanding. The culture in the United States, for example, is one of self-expression. Americans in general are used to voicing what they think or feel. They tend to speak their minds and express their opinions forthrightly and passionately, whether they love or hate something, whether "this is fabulous" or "this sucks." In other cultures, especially in Europe, people's first priority is not to express themselves but to understand. So if you do a sales presentation in Europe and people look very serious or puzzled and are not responding, most likely they're fully engaged and trying to understand how what you're presenting works. In the United States, silence might mean that your listeners are out to lunch while in Europe it might mean that your listeners are fully involved.

Rules (implicit vs. explicit, rigid vs. flexible, formal vs. improvised). Are rules or norms clearly defined or left fuzzy? Are rules fixed or can they be changed? Does a prepared meeting agenda need to be followed or can one deviate from it? Do people tend to comply with or deviate from agreements? What is the role of government and of unions?

In Sweden and the Netherlands, people take promises very seriously. In these countries, if people promise something, they intend to deliver no matter what. They will do anything to avoid the disgrace of failing to deliver on their promises. This leads them to be cautious, understandably, in making promises beyond what is predictable. In other cultures, such as in Latin America and China, people might make promises or agreements more easily but be less married to actually keeping them. In China, as we saw above, saying "yes" does not necessarily mean what it means in the United States, since in China other values (loyalty or contextual considerations such as the background in which the "yes" was uttered) might weigh more than the promise itself.

The United States' strong legal culture and tendency to litigate are well known. In other cultures, such as in Switzerland, people in general are more reluctant to use the courts to resolve disputes. If possible, the Swiss prefer to use informal gentlemen's agreements. The contracts they do use are minimal: a U.S. contract might be twenty-five pages long while the equivalent Swiss contract might only be ten pages.

Cultures can have vastly different rules based on their histories and legal traditions. Britain, for example, unlike Switzerland or the United States, does not have a no-fault divorce law. Under current British law, divorces are granted only under one of five categories, including adultery and abandonment. About half of the cases fall into a category called "unreasonable behavior," in which one party accuses the other of acting in a way that has made living together intolerable. And boy, does that lead to some interesting accusations, to say the least. In one case, a woman sued for divorce claiming that her husband insisted she dress and speak in the language of a

Klingon character from *Star Trek*. Then there's the man whose wife "would without justification flirt with any builder or tradesman, inappropriately touching them and declaring that she could not stop herself." Or the petition claiming "the respondent is unreasonably demanding sex every night from the petitioner, which is causing friction between the parties." Other complaints were about husbands with atrocious body odor and husbands who changed TV channels too fast. One petition read: "The respondent insisted that his pet tarantula, Timmy, sleep in a glass next to the matrimonial bed."[93]

This goes to show that cultural rules and norms can reach into physical wellbeing or sexuality. What is permissible in a given culture? Complimenting a female colleague on her attractive sweater might be perfectly acceptable in France; the same compliment can lead to sexual harassment charges in the United States. How strict are the norms on people's diet? In Italy and Japan, traditional foods are considered among the healthiest in the world, yet people smoke like chimneys. In the United States, smoking is typically frowned upon, but dietary norms are among the loosest in the world (nutrition writers use the acronym SAD for Standard American Diet to describe how Americans eat).

Time (short-term vs. long-term, past vs. future, single-tasking vs. multitasking). Do people have a short or long time-horizon for decisions? Is age seen as positive (wisdom) or negative (outdated)? Are people punctual or not? How "dead" are deadlines? Is time seen as a malleable commodity or as fixed? In India, many people have an eternal and slow sense of time. When I lived in Bombay, I found the Indian movies to be excruciatingly slow. If you were to make a promo video for a South Asian audience, it would have to reflect this slow pace. At the opposite extreme is the United States, where visuals and communications happen at a very high speed. The bottom line: if you do business with other cultures, adjust your pace.

Below we will see a real-world application of the Global Integrator™. But before I forget: you can use the Global Integrator™ not only to decode country cultures, but also company cultures. For example, after the DaimlerChrysler merger in 1998, the Chrysler unit had a much lower level of formality than Daimler, where most people addressed each other with the formal Sie. Daimler was much more hierarchical and more long-term oriented. These culture clashes were never resolved and contributed to the failure of the merger.

An Example: United States vs. India

The example below was created and written by my student at Columbia University, Maria Thomas, who is of Indian descent. It is, of course, highly subjective—the same disclaimer as above applies: all dimensions and ratings are generalizations and only approximate reality—but it is very perceptive and nicely illustrates the Global Integrator™ model.

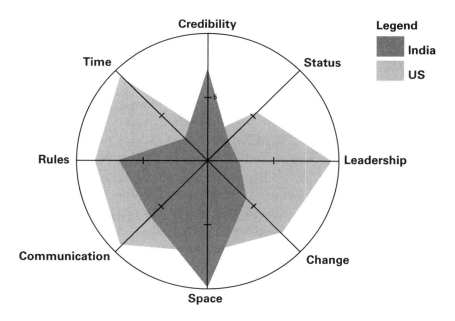

Global Integrator™, India vs. United States. By permission of Maria Thomas

Credibility (US: 2, India: 7) The work culture in the United States is definitely more result-driven than relationship-driven. The widely romanticized concept of the American Dream would never have survived in a nation that was not a meritocracy. In India, although results are acknowledged and may result in rewards and promotions up to a certain point, there exists a fair amount of cronyism, nepotism, etc., and the favored in-groups scale the ranks more rapidly than those who are not well-connected to those in power. This is especially true in business empires that are family legacies, as well as in politics and bureaucracies.

Status (US: 5, India: 2) Although there is a fairly clear delineation of duties in the United States, and hierarchy is present in that sense, there is none of the hushed reverence and unquestioning deference to authority that is a stock feature of many hierarchy-heavy Indian companies.

Leadership (US: 9, India: 2) The work culture in the United States is characterized by individualism. I think this is both part of the Cartesian legacy and the infiltration of the free-market mindset where efficient outcomes are expected to follow naturally from individual initiative and each respective player functioning in a way that maximizes his or her gains. There seems to be a sense that using one's comparative advantage will translate into some sort of societal collective advantage.

More emphasis is placed on team work and consensus-building in India. Given its staggering diversity and the fact that it is the world's largest democracy and needs to keep potentially volatile political and work situations at bay in order to move ahead, this is no surprise. Consensus is the only way India can keep its social and professional fabric intact.

Change (US: 8, India: 3) The brave new world of U.S. entrepreneurs is far less risk-averse than their counterparts anywhere else in the world. The United States has often been typecast as the land of opportunity and adventure. It is possible that this kind of stereotyping stems from proven real-world examples of

Americans being less resistant to change and more open to taking chances. On the whole, India is not as risk-friendly as the United States. There is a trend of upwardly mobile young professionals and entrepreneurs in the country taking more risks than their predecessors who would have adhered more closely to tried and tested business methods. But these are a privileged, educated cross-section of the Indian population and the more traditional establishments still seem wary of change.

Space (US: 7, India: 10) I have always found it fascinating to compare the differences between what is considered the appropriate distance one should keep when talking with someone, across different cultures. I've noticed that the acceptable distance in the United States is less than that in the United Kingdom for example, where a more decorous distance is kept. British people tend to be more protective of their physical space than Americans. Indians, on the other hand, show a happy disregard for space considerations. Arguably, this is a survival mechanism to deal with its burgeoning population of over a billion. If one were to have a problem with personal space encroachments in India, life would prove quite a challenge. The experience of traveling by train in peak-hour traffic in Mumbai where one has merely to stand on the station platform to be swept along with the swelling tide of people into a train (and hopefully it's the one you want), is one that quickly dispels any attachment to personal space because, quite frankly, it's a non-option. And this kind of experience is replicated not just on the commute to and from work, but in the quarters one stays in, in the market place, and at festivals and social gatherings.

Communication (US: 9, India: 6) The U.S. work culture revolves around an ethic of self-expression. Americans tend to be forthcoming with opinions and suggestions and there is a certain directness of approach. In India, although written and verbal communication are important, this is sometimes overshadowed by respect for hierarchy. In addition, some venues are not considered an appropriate place in which to speak one's mind. Similarly, it is seen as brazen effrontery if one were to openly disagree with a superior. Communication is more formalized and protocol-driven in India.

Rules (US: 8, Rules: 6) Rules in the United States are quite explicit. In India, companies often have unwritten rules dictated by internal politics. Many rules are more implicit in India, as they are more reliant on cultural understanding than a corporate guidebook.

Time (US: 9, India: 2) At least in its large cities, the United States displays a fast pace of work and life. Communication and action happen with remarkable, sometimes dizzying, celerity. The Indian attitude seems to be more fatalistic, relaxed, and loose when it comes to time considerations, deadlines, and pace.

Chapter Seven

Leading Across Cultures: The Global Leader Pyramid™

He says to her: "Honey, je t'adore."
She shoots back: "No, you shut the door!"

Tool 5: Global Leader Pyramid™

The fifth and final tool is the Global Leader Pyramid™ below. It is a simple and effective model for producing results in a cross-cultural environment, preventing cross-cultural mistakes in executing projects, and/or troubleshooting if and when mistakes occur. To build any successful accomplishment, you need to make sure that four levels are fulfilled: relationship, vision, strategy, and action. The Global Leader Pyramid™ has helped our clients maximize global results, navigate pitfalls, and minimize costs in cross-cultural projects. (In fact, my book *Leadership in 100 Days* is based entirely on the Global Leader Pyramid™.94)

A disclaimer is in order: any model of reality, much like a map, simplifies that reality. Many of the characterizations of cultures that follow are flagrant generalizations. Of course there are always exceptions to the rule, but generalizations can be very useful. In fact, generalization is the essence of culture: enough people act or think in a certain way that it becomes a general tendency. But please remember that cultures are only tendencies, and tools like the Global Integrator™ or the Global Leader Pyramid™ only approximate, never fully reflect reality.

Building Global Results

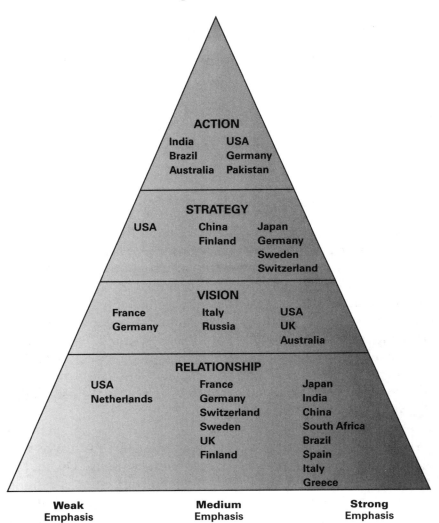

| Weak | Medium | Strong |
| Emphasis | Emphasis | Emphasis |

In order to produce an accomplishment of size, a project must move through four stages: relationship, vision, strategy and action. National and regional culture differ in their emphasis on these levels. If managers fail to respect the cultural emplasis on a particular level, cultures will inevitably clash. (Note: countries are chosen as illustrations only, and represent approximations of real situations.)
© 2001 Swiss Consulting Group, Inc.

Relationship

The first and fundamental level of the Pyramid is Relationship—and that is true in any culture in the world, but some emphasize Relationship much more than others do. In most regions of the United States, relationship is less important than in other cultures, such as Japan, Chile, or Saudi Arabia. You remember my war stories above, when I lived in India and Japan. For example, when the chief executive of my client invited me to accompany him to the bathhouse, it was a breakthrough in our relationship. It was important for him to develop the trust between us before getting down to business.

In Western cultures, by contrast, people downplay or simply ignore relationship building. They go beyond the relationship quickly, to Vision or Strategy or worst of all, directly to Action. They are so hungry for results that they forget that Relationship—including partnership, team spirit, shared interests, shared values, and trust—is the foundation for all accomplishment. If you can deepen and broaden the foundation of Relationship with others, you increase the height of the Pyramid you can build. In other words, the deeper the relationship, the greater the possible accomplishment. At this ground level of the Pyramid, you ask, "Who are you?" and "Who are we?"

Relationship is the key to effective leadership in all cultures. Whether you want to make a strategic sale, enhance performance of your team, or enter a market, you simply cannot succeed unless you build and cultivate relationships marked by mutual trust, common interests, and open communication. In some cultures, Relationship matters even more than in others. In the BRICS countries we covered above, as well as in other emerging-market nations, commanding sufficient "Vitamin B" ("B" for the German word for Relationship, *Beziehung*) is often the crucial common denominator for great wealth. Why? While some of these countries have robust capital markets and economic organizations like those in Europe and North America, they may lack the same political and legal institutions and traditions. Deal makers and entrepreneurs can leverage these gaps by building relationships with the government that give them anything from better business contracts to outright control of entire markets. In China, for example, these government ties are even formalized as the government picks winners and losers in a type of state-sponsored capitalism.

Such privileged relationships pay off: in 2012 the seventy richest delegates to China's National People's Congress were worth an aggregate of $89.8 billion. Additionally, children of Communist Party officials have often moved into important industry positions: when Wen Yunsong, the son of the former Chinese premier Wen Jiabao, was appointed chairman of the China Satellite Communications Company in early 2012, the company's stock promptly rose by almost 50 percent.

In Africa, Uhuru Kenyatta, the son of Kenya's first president Jomo Kenyatta, served as deputy prime minister and is one of the continent's richest residents. In the Mideast, the Bin Laden family built its wealth with construction contracts for the Saudi government it got from its close relationship with Saudi royals.[95] But ultimately it is true for any culture: nothing helps like friends in high places.

Vision

Once you have a deep enough relationship, the next level of the Pyramid is Vision. What is the bigger picture that you and I are committed to? Before you have aligned on that shared vision, delving into Strategy or Action is risky: either you and your colleagues will not pull in the same direction, or your Strategy will simply be an extension of the past into the future, rather than emanating from the future. At the Vision level, you ask: "What are we here for?"

One culture that is quite visionary is the one in the United States. Americans in general tend to be optimistic about the future, see a new future as an adventure, and be open to creating a bold Vision. Another culture that tends to love vision (as opposed to Action to implement Vision) is the British culture. If you negotiate with Britons, you might find that they like to keep brainstorming and exploring, and to be reluctant to go into Strategy or Action. They love to flirt and hate to f . . . ahem, jump into bed.

Continental Europeans, on the other hand, have a tendency to be skeptical of Vision—not surprisingly, given their long history of grand visions that ended disastrously, from Napoleon to Hitler. The revered former German chancellor Helmut Schmidt went as far as counseling that "People who have a vision should go see a doctor." While Americans tend to commit the blunder of jumping from the Vision to the Action level, Europeans tend to make another mistake: they leave Vision too quickly and move immediately to Strategy by asking, "But how do we do this? I don't see that this can be done" or "We tried that five years ago and it was a disaster." The German head of an American company's European subsidiary went to a global meeting where his American bosses and peers advocated a vision of increasing profits from $300 million to $1 billion within a year, an admittedly ambitious, if not outlandish, goal. The German president could not see the strategy and immediately nixed the project without allowing a full, uncensored conversation for possibility.

Strategy

The third level of the pyramid is Strategy. Once you have built the partnership and aligned on a common future that all key stakeholders are committed to, you then must build the Strategy to make your Vision a reality. Now it is entirely appropriate, even crucial, to ask, "How do we get there?" Now it is time for the skeptics and critics to speak up. You deal with people's concerns about how to do it, what to do if something does not work, and what could go wrong. You build feasibility (including action plans, timelines, roles and accountabilities, and budgets), manage risk, set the priorities, and say "No" to lesser priorities. Only when you have the strategy do you go into Action, the top level.

Some cultures, including those of Germany, Switzerland, and Japan, strongly emphasize the How of Strategy. Some overdo it: one extreme example is the Japanese company Matsushita, which reportedly operates from a 250-year plan. The potential pitfall is obvious: you can become enslaved by a rigid plan that prevents you from seizing opportunities.

But as we have seen, the Strategy level is crucial for results, the How needs to be clear, and it needs to be owned by a broad base of your people. How do you create ownership in Strategy? Include key stakeholders from across the enterprise, from all international subsidiaries or affiliates, perhaps even global alliance or joint venture partners, in meetings to create Strategy and policies, or to make other decisions that will affect their operations. Begin these meetings by achieving a shared understanding, and stay with it until a consensus has been reached. This alignment will allow you to operate effectively for one year (or less in a fast-changing industry). Be sensitive to when the next meeting is needed to create the Strategy, policies, and operating agreements for the next cycle. In between these major meetings, use occasional conference calls or videoconferences to sustain the relationship and handle any issues that arise. Be willing to invest in co-creation with your international stakeholders. The investment may seem expensive, even nerve-racking, but the return is handsome. I learned this many years ago as director of global operations for an international organization, and global affiliates increased revenue by 500 percent in five years while holding expenses stable, once we had created an environment of strong Relationship, Vision, and Strategy.

Action

As we saw above, one mistake Americans often make is to launch into Action too quickly, before the Relationship is clear and the Strategy is created. They are confident that "Just Do It" will provide learning-by-doing. In addition, they tend to manage by objectives and often have urgent deadlines to meet. They have to produce the results by the end of the quarter or the week. But going into Action too quickly robs people of a fuller understanding of the whole strategy.

People in some countries such as Germany and Switzerland must first understand how they are going to get things done. Unless the How is clear to them, they often resist getting into Action. In Switzerland and Germany, Nike's slogan "Just Do It" just doesn't do it. They want to think things through and then take action. That way of being can, of course, lead to other pitfalls. Germans may get so attached to a certain action or set of procedures that they cannot stop what they are doing, even if it is strategically wrong or does not work anymore. The German president above was known for sticking with well-established pathways and opposing innovative ideas that had yet to prove valid.

The Global Results Pyramid™ is ideal for quick diagnosis and troubleshooting in Action. If people are upset or don't speak up, for instance, you can bet that Relationship is insufficient or lacking altogether. If people are not clear about the future, if they are not aligned, or if they are resigned to the past and think "same as it ever was," that is when a shared inspiring Vision is missing. If people are undecided or confused, if they don't know what to do, or if they have concerns, Strategy is missing. And finally, if people fail to keep their agreements, what's missing is action, in particular specificity about the Action and clear deadlines.

But usually, weak Action is merely a symptom of the fact that other floors of the Pyramid are missing or built shoddily. For example, if there is a lack of compliance with one of your policies in global subsidiaries, chances are you did not build sufficient Relationship with the people involved, or they never owned the Strategy or rationale behind the policy in the first place. Go back to how the policy originated. Did the subsidiaries or affiliates have a voice in its shaping, or were they simply expected to adopt and abide by it? And before the Strategy, did people own the Vision underlying the strategy? Are they clear on the purpose underlying it? Is it a common future, or is it the Vision of only a few executives in a closed boardroom at global headquarters? (This is just a cursory illustration; the Global Leader Pyramid Poster™ is designed to help teams troubleshoot projects quickly through a diagnosis along the Pyramid.[96])

Lab: Sweeping Generalizations on Doing Business in Europe

Now, using what you have learned from the Onion Model, the Global Integrator™ and the Global Leader Pyramid™, you can apply these tools to your target culture. The table below gives examples of business cultures and preferences in North, Central, and South Europe in areas such as building credibility, change management, or performance management. Again, they are highly subjective and for illustration only; I call them "sweeping generalizations."

Now that you have the basic intercultural tools under your belt, we can move on to how companies foster a global mindset and how they base their innovation strategy on being "glocal." This is the focus of the next chapter.

Area	North (e.g., United Kingdom, Scandinavia)	Central (e.g., German-speakers)	South/West (e.g., France, Southern Europe)
Presentation	Wit, irony, sarcasm. Low-key, reserved. Self-deprecating humor; avoid self-promotion or blowing their own horn. Skeptical toward leaders	Facts. Want to understand (instead of expressing themselves). Give good and bad news; criticism. No surprises. Modesty, humility.	"We are the cradle of civiliza-tion, we are smarter." Intellectual and emotional. Arguments. Relationship more important than data.
Change	Tradition. Long time horizon. A new idea must be their idea. Love to flirt . . . (vision, but reluctant to sign on the dotted line).	Technocratic, pragmatic, rational. You need them to make things work. Ritualistic. Attached to pathway, process, and rules.	Change must be their idea. Debating, know-it-all. Provocative to test your resolve.
Credibility	Tend to see USA as an overly dom-inant bully. Affiliation and history matter.	Statistics, numbers. Hard work. Status, hierarchy.	Suspicious of USA. Passion, masculinity. Elders are seen as wiser. Better poor and smart than rich and stupid.
Business/ Customer Relations	Be patient. Don't be seen as "hungry."	Customer seen as disruption of the quality process. Punctual. Get to work.	Relationship matters more than skills. They may test your credulity.
Meeting Protocol	Class is still important (the Royals, "old money"). Let them dictate the agenda and pace.	Don't waste time. They know how to run it. They have been around the block.	Class is still important. Focus on relationship, don't push for business too quickly. Have fun.

Area	North (e.g., United Kingdom, Scandinavia)	Central (e.g., German-speakers)	South/West (e.g., France, Southern Europe)
Negotiations	Beware of legalism. Do not micro-manage. Refer to US-UK "special relation-ship" (Churchill).	Take care of the details. "Selling is cheap."	Debate. Don't get hooked by their com-plaints.
Communication/ Training	Indirect feedback. Sarcasm or dark humor.	Direct. Functional. Honest. Formal. Sometimes philosophical.	Complaints. Passion.
Entertaining	Sophisticated. Style. Class.	Dress code: "Be poor to be good." Avoid pomp (Protestant or Lutheran frugality).	Lavish. Connoisseurs. "Savoir vivre." Physical.
Management/ Subordinate Approaches	Sympathy for the underdog. "Beat the system."	Fear of leadership. Obedient to hierarchy. Labor-manage-ment partnership. Compliance with rules is important.	Autocratic legacy in Spain, Italy, Greece.
Employee Performance	Less goal- or reward-oriented. Let them decide, but hold them to account.	Strong compliance. Clear expectations. Once they commit, they deliver. Awkward with praise.	Weak compliance. Need specific agreements, instructions. Do not accuse.

Table: Sweeping Generalizations on Doing Business in Europe

Chapter Eight

Cross-Cultural Strategy as an Asset for Innovation

The greatest need for leadership is in the dark . . .
It is when the system is changing so rapidly . . .
that old prescriptions and old wisdoms can only lead to
catastrophe and leadership is necessary to call people|to
the very strangeness of the new world being born.
Kenneth Boulding

French Intellectuals to be Deployed in Afghanistan to Convince Taliban of Non-Existence of God[97]

For Immediate Release: February 2002

The clean-up portion of the ground war in Afghanistan heated up yesterday when the Allies revealed plans to airdrop a platoon of crack French existentialist philosophers into the country to destroy the morale of the remaining Taliban zealots by proving the non-existence of God.

Elements from the feared Jean-Paul Sartre Brigade, or "Black Berets," will be parachuted into the combat zones to spread doubt, despondency, and existential anomie among the enemy. Hardened by numerous intellectual battles fought during their long occupation of Paris's Left Bank, their first action will be to establish a number of sidewalk cafes at strategic points near the front lines.

There they will drink coffee and talk animatedly about the absurd nature of life and man's lonely isolation in the universe. They will be accompanied by a number of heartbreakingly beautiful girlfriends who will further spread dismay by sticking their tongues in the philosophers' ears every five minutes and look-ing remote and unattainable to everyone else.

Their leader, Colonel Marc-Ange Belmondo, spoke yester-day of his confidence in the success of their mission. Sorbonne graduate Belmondo, a very intense and unshaven young man in a black pullover, gesticulated wildly and said, "The Taliban are caught in a logical fallacy of the most ridiculous. There is no God and I can prove it. Take your tongue out of my ear, Juliet, I am talking."

Mr. Belmondo plans to deliver an impassioned thesis on man's nauseating freedom of action with special reference to the work of Foucault and the films of Alfred Hitchcock.

However, humanitarian agencies have been quick to con-demn the operation as inhumane, pointing out that the effects of passive smoking from the Frenchmen's endless Gitanes could wreak a terrible toll on civilians in the area.

Previous chapters have covered cross-cultural savvy at an indi-vidual level. Now we come to the pinnacle of the book: har-nessing cross-cultural strategy as an *organizational* asset (of course not like in the example above). This chapter focuses on how enterprises can build truly global cultures that spur ideas, innovation, and knowledge management on a global scale, and where cultures are not obstacles but vital opportunities for growth and championship performance.

From Multinational to *Metanational:* Searching for Innovation Globally

Yves Doz, the Solvay Chaired Professor of Technological Innovation at INSEAD, argues that most multinationals fail to harvest the most precious resources—ideas and innovation— from the far-flung regions in which they operate, and they will suffer for it. Doz has suggested a new type of global corporation attuned to the dynamics of the knowledge economy: the "meta-national." He and his co-authors José Santos and Peter Williamson describe the metanational as "a company that builds a new kind of competitive advantage by discovering, accessing, mobilizing, and leveraging knowledge from many locations around the world."

One of the problems with innovation is that it rarely starts in headquarters, since most managers there have precious little incentive to disrupt the status quo. Why? Simple: the status quo is what keeps these managers where they are—at the top of the heap. Why should they endorse innovation? They will likely see any change as risky or threatening their power or perks. They have the most to lose from innovation.

So if not from headquarters, where do breakthrough ideas come from? The answer is, not from the global office but from the periphery. But truth be told, very few CEOs see that, let alone run their companies consistent with it. This misconception has led to countless missed opportunities. To most managers, becoming a global company still means to penetrate markets around the world. A traditional multinational develops a stan-dard product for its home market, and then sells, or, in Doz's words, "projects" that standard around the world. But the old model of the traditional multinational has run out of steam for at least three reasons. One is knowledge dispersion: the days when a single country like the United States or a single location like Silicon Valley was the sole place where innovation came from are gone. Now breakthrough ideas come from more and more places around the world.

Secondly, Doz and his colleagues argue that traditional multinationals have missed out on the real potential offered by globalization. They have used (or abused) global markets to find ever-cheaper labor in far-flung places. And third, they have pushed their products into new markets without differentiating those products from the ones they sell in their home market (old product / new market).

Perhaps most perniciously, traditional multinationals have been intellectually arrogant, adopting a mindset that "we know best" and pretty much forcing their global subsidiaries to follow the rules, norms, and practices imposed on them by headquarters. But companies that are too deep in a projection mode tend to ignore too much available knowledge from peripheral locations. The result: they leave money on the table.

The demands of the knowledge economy are turning this strategy on its head, Doz says. Today, the challenge is to innovate by listening on a global scale and *learning from the world.* And because innovation drives growth, those companies that fail to learn will be left behind.

Doz and his colleagues define the metanational by three core capabilities: being the first to identify and capture new knowledge emerging all over the world, mobilizing this globally scattered knowledge to out-innovate competitors, and turning this innovation into value by producing, marketing, and delivering efficiently on a global scale.

Which companies meet the criteria of the metanational? According to Doz, no company is a fully fledged metanational yet, but players like Nestlé and Amazon.com have clearly moved in this direction. Amazon adopted a multi-domestic strategy, building separate subsidiaries and supply chains in key markets. Nestlé's Singapore operation kept in close touch with local customers. Its R&D center had the task of monitoring quality assurance for Nestlé suppliers in the Far East, ensuring that all input products met Nestlé standards—very much a traditional multinational function, but this close attention to suppliers allowed it to keep a finger on the pulse of new market needs and new technologies in those suppliers. Nestlé used its global R&D activity to build a magnet for dispersed knowledge. It built Nestec, a separate company that coordinated innovation by combining R&D knowledge with sensitivity to emerging market needs around the world. A twenty-person team acted as knowledge brokers by putting "customers" (the operating units) in touch with the right "suppliers" (drawn from Nestlé's Technological Development Centers in Switzerland, Germany, France, England, Sweden, Italy, Spain, the United States, Ecuador, Singapore, and the Ivory Coast) to serve specific R&D projects. Nestec took charge of specific deliverables and charged a fee.[98]

How can companies leverage globalization and learn from the world? "Our argument is that there are three core steps," Doz said in an interview;[99] "a step of *sensing,* which is identifying and accessing existing knowledge; a step we call *mobilizing,* which is integrating scattered capabilities and emerging market opportunities in new products and services; and then we stress a third step, which is *optimizing operations* to maximize the return on these new offerings."

The key is to no longer assume that the relevant knowledge lies exclusively in your home base, but to accept the fact that peripheral locations can generate not only best practices but also innovation that has the power to bring about entrepreneurial leaps if harnessed correctly.

The role of management in metanationals is to find and link the best ideas from all the company's locations. This may not involve fundamental changes in the day-to-day operations of sales forces, manufacturing plants, or even traditional R&D labs. But the slogan "Think global, act local" now needs to be turned around: "Think local, act global." Thinking local means, "We are going to leverage our local capabilities globally, in a much more effective way." The game is no longer to leverage your global capabilities locally. "It is a change of mindset, a change of attitude, and a change of perspective," Doz says.

How do you do this? You would appoint "ambassadors" or "explorers" whose job is to listen for best practices and scout for innovative ideas in far-flung locations, and then share these practices and ideas across geographic entities worldwide. People who take this role need to be curious about new ideas instead of pushing existing ideas; they need the social competencies to rub shoulders with customers and suppliers and others in distant markets or plants or labs; and they need to be strategic enough to sense new trends in consumer behavior and then connect the dots in a larger picture.

One top manager who served as such an ambassador was Jack Welch when he still led General Electric. He would clock some 200,000 miles a year to visit GE locations around the world. Whenever he heard or found out about a relevant idea or practice, he would immediately post it on the company's intranet or send a broadcast email to all GE employees to make that knowledge available to them.

Another tool of the metanational can be strategic alliances, provided you use the alliance not just for projecting your agenda, but for learning. Sony Music used minority ownerships in various European independent labels. This kept it abreast of emerging trends and talents. "The French–Italian chip company STMicroelectronics is an example of a company that cultivates multiple alliances with customers and uses them actively for learning," says Doz. "One of the largest Portuguese groups, Sonae, focuses on supermarkets and shopping mall development. That's not very high-tech global stuff, but they have a very clearly articulated strategy of using alliances. It's a way for them, first, to learn new businesses, and second, to acquire new knowledge from different national communities, in order to expand their existing businesses internationally."

The bottom line is that your home base is not the only source of innovation. You can garner innovation from the world. That is when cross-cultural savvy becomes a strategic asset for your firm.

Now let's compare two cases of what can go wrong, and right, when companies aim to think local: Coca-Cola in China and Pepsico in India.

Coke in China: What Went Wrong (and Right)?

In 2009 China's government rejected Coca-Cola's planned $2.3 billion acquisition of the Chinese company Huiyuan Juice. Huiyuan, based in Beijing and the largest privately-owned juice company in China, would have given Coke much-needed market penetration in the country's third- and fourth-tier cities. Most companies that go into China target Shanghai and Beijing, ignoring less-developed areas because they think consumers there are too poor to buy high-priced foreign goods. The reality is that these areas are home to 800 million Chinese consumers moving into the middle class. What's more, the Chinese government offered these consumers a 13 percent rebate on home appliances like televisions, refrigerators, and air conditioners to boost their consumption.

Coke made a smart move: it sought access to those emerging markets, arguably the next great battleground for business where the real consumer growth will come in the next decade.[100] So far so good. But more metanational savvy might have prevented Coke's failed attempt to acquire Huiyuan. One lesson is that companies must look long and hard at China's legislation. Foreigners complain that those laws are often opaque and whimsically interpreted by local officials, but in fact the laws governing major purchases are fairly straightforward. As Chinalawblog.com summed them up, "Foreigners are permitted to purchase non-majority interests in strong, successful Chinese companies, but only if there is some added benefit, such as transfer of technology, advanced management, or access to foreign markets."

Nonetheless, China is moving toward greater competition. It is wary of monopolies and is trying to build more national corporate champions like the appliance-maker Haier and the sports apparel firm Li Ning. The official justification of the deal's rejection was that it would reduce competition, since Huiyuan already controls 8.5 percent of the country's fruit and vegetable juice market and 40 percent of its pure juice market; Coke already commands more than half of China's soft drink market and 12 percent of its fruit and vegetable juice market.

Coca-Cola thought the government wouldn't mind the sale of a nonstrategic asset, but a simple reading of the relevant Chinese laws would have shown that the government doesn't want foreign firms to buy controlling stakes in large national players that don't need financial or management help.

The other trend Coke ignored because of a missing meta-national mindset was this: in a country where tainted food scares and pollution problems plague daily life, younger consumers willingly shell out for products they think are good for them. A Chinese market research firm found that younger consumers are willing to pay 20-30 percent more for premium construction materials for their unfinished homes.[101] DuPont has capitalized on that trend by providing Chinese homeowners with home construction and decoration products and/or services that emphasize health and safety. The company charges more than its native competitors, but it is driving major growth in China by catering to younger consumers who demand healthy and safe products.

Pepsi: Repairing a Poisoned Reputation in India

Even as companies begin to take the mantra of social responsibility seriously, they find themselves more vulnerable to politically charged onslaughts. Pepsi's ongoing battle over water in India[102] illustrates an escalating global backlash against the ways multinationals consume natural resources. The hostility towards Pepsi in India has been exacerbated by the particular meaning water holds for Indians: bathing in it can be a sacred act. For millions, a ritual bath in the Ganges River is a defining moment in their lives, and death is not properly marked until the ashes are scattered in the Ganges. In a global poll last year by consumer research group Henley World about the main things people do to improve their well-being, Americans reported taking dietary supplements; Germans cited sunbathing; Indians listed drinking water.

The issue touched a raw nerve as Indian government studies had reported high pesticide levels in milk, rice, and other staples, raising concerns about toxins seeping into the water supply. Indians rely heavily on groundwater not just for drinking but also for agriculture; they have drilled an estimated 21 million wells, most unregulated, since 1965.

Pepsi's water clash in India took a dramatic turn after PepsiCo executive Abhiram Seth visited Sunita Narain, a well-known activist in New Delhi, in February, 2003. The meeting was quite a clash of minds. At the time, Narain was age 45 and highly outspoken; she stemmed from a family of freedom fighters who had supported Mahatma Gandhi in his quest for India's independence in the 1940s. She idolized her father even though (or perhaps because) he did not always comply with Gandhi's creed of nonviolence and, she said, "I'm told he even made bombs." Seth was a fifty-one-year-old, chatty, wry manager who served as Pepsi's chief navigator through the complex regulatory and political channels of his native country. As executive director of exports and external affairs, he also managed the eclectic agricultural projects that held the potential to help improve Pepsi's image. Seth came to Narain's plant-filled New Delhi office just after her organization had tested the country's top ten bottled-water brands for pesticides and was pressing for tighter government regulation. He came, he explained in an interview later, "to understand the data and see if we could work together to address the issues."

Narain recalls it differently. She claims that Seth bullied her and "gave me a huge lecture about nationalism or some rubbish . . . He was clearly trying to get me to back off." With Aquafina scoring near the top in bottled water quality in the country, she wondered whether there was some broader agenda at work. Narain suspected Pepsi didn't want tougher standards for water because that might require more rigorous treatment of the water going into its sodas. Naturally suspicious of corporate behavior, she thought: "Why don't we check their soft drinks?"

Pepsi executives were stunned and outraged. "When you're testing in subparts per billion," Seth recalled, "it's like measuring one second in 320 years." Pepsi's India team immediately got on the phone with Indra K. Nooyi, then president and chief financial officer, and Michael White, PepsiCo International's CEO. "We took it very seriously," says White, "but we also knew our products were completely safe."

Nooyi, now Pepsico's chief executive, said in a later interview that she still felt guilty filling a bathtub with water. It sounds far-fetched coming from the chief executive of a major multinational corporation, until you consider her early years. She didn't get much water growing up during the 1960s in the Indian coastal city of Chennai. Although she describes her family as "very middle class," they had to rise every morning between three and five—the only hours that the valves to the municipal water supply were turned on—and fill every bucket in the house. Two buckets were set aside for cooking, and two each would go to Nooyi, her older sister, and her younger brother. "You had to think about whether to take a bath," says Nooyi, matter-of-factly. "You learned to live your life off those two buckets."

Nooyi had left Chennai propelled by a dream to build a career in the United States. She headed to the prestigious Indian Institute of Management and later Yale University before moving into the corporate sphere, eventually settling at PepsiCo in 1994. When she was named CEO in October 2006, India's water again became a focus of her life.

Pepsi did something highly unusual: it held a rare joint press conference with Coke in New Delhi, offering data that contradicted Narain's and saying the company followed the same strict standards all around the world. But protesters in Mumbai and Kolkata defaced Pepsi and Coke ads and burned placards depicting soda bottles. Several states restricted or banned soda sales. Blasted with e-mail alerts from Narain's organization, journalists and bloggers worldwide leapt on the story, raising the specter of a global consumer reaction just when soda makers were coming under harsh scrutiny for contributing to obesity.

Nooyi said later that Indians' sensitivity to both water quality and foreign companies made Pepsi an inviting target. But she admitted that the company's marketing strategy had made matters worse. Rather than promote the company's efforts to improve water and crops, Pepsi had run splashy ads bursting with Indian celebrities. It painted titanic versions of its red, white, and blue logo on ancient Himalayan rocks and buildings around the country. "Combine the public seeing the mercenary side of us, along with the fact that this was an American company," she says, "they didn't see the other things we were doing."

After another study by Narain's group, the southern state of Kerala banned the manufacture and sale of all Coke and Pepsi products while other states cut soft-drink sales in schools, colleges, and hospitals. "Everyone carried the story, especially on TV," Seth recalled with a sigh. Protests revved up again with some demonstrators pouring cola down the throats of donkeys to show that the drink was unfit for humans. Sales dipped as Narain's campaign again played to the conflicted attitude that Indian consumers have toward powerful foreign brands—especially those portrayed as profiting at their expense.

One of Nooyi's first priorities as CEO was a trip to India, where she spoke widely about Pepsi's initiatives to improve water and the environment, as well as her own fond memories of growing up in the country. One of her main themes: "This is a company with a soul." Indian newspapers and television covered her tour lavishly and with praise. Soda sales improved, although they ended 2006 flat compared with rapid double-digit growth in China. While the worst of the pesticide scandal is behind Pepsi today, a cloud remains because the government still hasn't set contaminant standards. And all of this could have been prevented with a proactive metanational mindset and listening for cultural preferences before Pepsico's marketing effort.

Chapter Nine

The Acid Test:
Alliances and M&A

All men are caught in an inescapable network of mutuality, tied in a
single garment of destiny. Whatever affects one affects all indirectly . . .
I can never be what I ought to be until you are what you ought to be,
and you can never be what you ought to be until I am what I ought to be.
This is the interrelated structure of reality.

Martin Luther King, Jr.

A ship sank in high seas and the following people got stranded on a beautiful deserted island in the middle of nowhere:

A. Two Italian men and one Italian woman

B. Two French men and one French woman

C. Two German men and one German woman

D. Two Greek men and one Greek woman

E. Two Polish men and one Polish woman

F. Two Mexican men and one Mexican woman

G. Two Irish men and one Irish woman

H. Two American men and one American woman

I. Two Indian men and one Indian woman

One month later, on various parts of the island, the following was observed:

A. One Italian man killed the other Italian man for the Italian woman.

B. The two French men and the French woman are living happily together.

C. The two German men have a strict weekly schedule of when they alternate with the German woman.

D. The two Greek men are sleeping together and the Greek woman is cooking and cleaning for them.

E. The two Polish men took a long look at the endless ocean and a long look at the Polish woman, and they started swimming.

F. The two Mexican men are talking to all the other men on the island, trying to sell them the Mexican woman.

G. The two Irish men began joint adventures (again, of course not along the lines of the joke above) by dividing up their part of the island into Northern and Southern parts and setting up a distillery. They do not remember the Irish woman because it gets sort of foggy after the first few liters of coconut whiskey but at least the English are not getting any.

H. The two American men are contemplating suicide. The American woman is complaining about her body being her own, the true nature of feminism, how she can do everything they can do, about the necessity of fulfillment, the equal division of the household chores, how her last boyfriend respected her opinion and treated her much better, and how her relationship with her mother is improving.

I. The two Indian men are still waiting for someone to introduce them to the Indian woman.

Now that we have tools for maximizing cross-cultural results and learning while minimizing the "friction losses" (as one of our clients likes to call them), we can apply our knowledge to an area rich with cross-cultural failures: alliances, mergers, acquisitions, and joint ventures. Statistics tell us that more than half of attempted mergers and acquisitions fail, that only one-quarter of large-scale mergers succeed, and that a full 83 percent fail to improve shareholder value.[103] This goes even more for M&As that are cross-border. It is hardly necessary to cite examples. In addition to the DaimlerChrysler above, where the German Daimler executives dominated virtually every key position in the combined entity while Chrysler people had little if any say in its leadership, a much older example and one of the first is the failed joint venture of AT&T and Olivetti in the mid-1980s.

The American and Italian companies attempted a partnership for their computer and word processing products, with Olivetti manufacturing the products and AT&T marketing and selling them under the AT&T brand. Tapas Sen, a former senior AT&T executive, told me that "we didn't quite understand what it takes to do business with another culture. First, our team was not conversant in the Italian language, so we always depended on their understanding of English." But language was only one of the barriers to understanding. Neither company conducted a full needs analysis to understand the other side's primary agenda. The companies never quite clarified their mutual expectations with each other. The Italian Olivetti culture was massively different from AT&T's culture. The two companies did not get along and finally agreed to get a divorce.

When BMW merged with Rover, German managers opted for a hands-off management style for fear of stepping on the toes of their British counterparts. (Many Europeans are all too ready to see Germans as "Teutonic" command-and-control managers.) The kid gloves were the wrong move; the merger failed famously.

A Swedish-American pharmaceutical company ran into multiple lawsuits because senior managers in the United States reportedly withheld information from the Swedish executives when they asked them to move to the combined company's New Jersey offices. The company promised each Swede a U.S. Green Card; in fact they never intended to grant people resident status. The dispute was programmed into the merger; the result was a loss of trust and a significant brain drain, as many Swedish executives left the joint company.

Another Swedish-American M&A is the most recent example. In 1989 General Motors, together with Investor AB, acquired Saab; each owned 50 percent of the joint company. Eleven years later, in 2000, GM bought the other half, so Saab Automobiles became a wholly owned subsidiary of GM. Another decade later, GM spun Saab off to the Dutch entrepreneur Victor Muller, the former chief executive of sports-car maker Spyker Cars. In October 2011, Pang Da Automobile Trade and Zhejiang Youngman Lotus Automobile reached a tentative agreement to purchase Saab for $140 million, but the acquisition fell through when GM—which had effective veto power over any deal since it still owned key patents used by Saab—balked and Saab was forced to declare insolvency in December that year.[104]

Below we will review GE Capital's integration model as a useful method for integrating acquisitions, but even GE is not exempt from culture clashes in mergers. The company's former chairman Jack Welch's autocratic and aggressive style in negotiations with the EU competition authority was one of the causes of the GE/Honeywell merger's prohibition and failure back in 2001, wrote Michael Bonsignore, the former chief of Honeywell, in the *Financial Times.* Especially Welch's wrathful behavior vis-à-vis competition commissioner Mario Monti "was a case study in how not to handle process and protocol."[105] In a two-day meeting in Brussels just after 9/11, Welch made a last-ditch personal appeal to Monti to push for approval of the merger. When he realized that his plea left the commissioner unmoved, he angrily accused Monti of acting as "judge, jury, and prosecutor" and said Monti was "making up the rules as he goes along." He abruptly declared that he was leaving Brussels to work on his book. "That's good, Mr. Welch," Monti was quoted as saying with excruciating calm. "You can make this meeting your final chapter."[106]

We don't know if the clash between Monti and Welch was one of cultures—American vs. European—or of egos. What we do know is this: one international study[107] found that cultural integration had been the biggest challenge to a successful merger in the experiences of 150 corporate executives. The executive search firm Towers Perrin (now Towers Watson, itself the result of a 2007 merger, so it should know), in cooperation with the *Economist Intelligence Unit,* reported in a survey of 132 senior Fortune 500 executives that for more than half—57 percent—incompatible cultures had been the principal cause of a failed merger or acquisition they had been involved with.[108] Note that the latter study found no correlation between cultural distance and merger failure *per se,* but the real issue was how the merging firms had managed the process of *bridging* the cultural distance. In other words, cultural distance does not doom alliances, ignoring or underestimating it does.

When things work fine, alliances are wonderful. The question is, what do you do when there is a breakdown? Will you hold the line or will you default to some old behavior that worked once in the past but is now obsolete? In mergers and acquisitions, the same principles apply as in relationships: people tend to do to others the things they expect others to do to them. One problem is that we rarely express exactly what we expect. We avoid figuring out exactly what we want, when, how often, and from whom and if we do, we do not tell the other party, get a shared understanding, or follow up if the alliance or merger partner does not meet our implicit standards. The other problem, in B2B relationships and negotiations, just as in personal relationships, is the failure to stand in the shoes of the other party. All too often, leaders apply different standards to themselves, depending on their role in a particular business relationship. They are not willing to give their suppliers the trust they expect when they themselves are suppliers. If you are engaged in an M&A or strategic alliance yourself, or if you manage any relationships with buyers and/or suppliers, I want you to do another small exercise (yes, they *are* still good for you):

Lab.

In a workshop held outside London with railroad suppliers for the Chunnel, the tunnel connecting Britain and France, the suppliers were charged with building an integrated rail system on both the French and the English side. Naturally, there was a culture clash.

The British side didn't communicate as directly as the French side, and they thought the French unreliable. The French couldn't understand why the Brits avoided clear-cut deadlines and agreements, while the Brits thought the French were overly legalistic and impatient, to name but a few mutual opinions (or rather complaints). The workshop facilitators had the French and British firms split into breakout groups, whose assignment was to answer three simple questions on flipcharts: what are your concerns (or complaints) about the other side; what are your expectations of them; what are your promises to them?

The answers the two groups came up with gave them some clarity. But then came the clincher—they had to turn the tables and put themselves in the other side's shoes. On a different flipchart, they had to answer the same questions, but from the other side's perspective, as if this view were their own. Looking through the eyes of their alliance partners, what were *their* concerns, expectations, and promises? It was as if a veil had been lifted. They came back into the plenary and said, "Now I see why the other guys always complained about shoddy quality, about being on time, about being too rigid," etc.

This technique, which is a bit like that of actors who have to *become* the character they play (imagine how you would see the world if you were a murderer, a baker, or a general) works also with multiple groups.

The Australian subsidiary of a global pharmaceutical company wanted to improve its dealings with Asian cultures, from India to China to Korea; but more importantly, the Australians suffered from cultural clashes with Swiss headquarters, whose senior managers had never checked their assumptions (for example, about Australia being a saturated or even stagnant market, or Australians being notoriously lazy and on permanent vacation). No company CEO or chairman had ever come to Australia. The managing director first gave his Australian perspective on the Swiss headquarters. Then he acted out the Swiss perspective, saying in a deep and solemn voice, "We make ze rules; you must play by ze rules or we will have to punish you." The other partici-pants laughed so hard at his dour face and his bureaucratic tone of voice that they almost fell off their chairs. It was a revelation. Putting themselves in the shoes of the other side gave the com-pany vital intelligence for its strategy. The results: within nine months the Australian subsidiary was recognized as a champion performer within the firm. In the words of the managing director, his Australian team had "changed the prescription glasses" of how they were perceived by headquarters.

Pick one of your key, current or potential alliance partners or contractors, then answer the following questions: First, what are your specific expectations of the partner? What do you count on them for? What can they count on you for? Given your answers to these questions, what are your biggest questions still unanswered?

Second, see if you can stand in their shoes and embody them. This requires a great deal of empathy on your part. Try seeing what *their* specific expectations are of you. What is most important to them? What can they count on you for? Given the answers to these questions, what are their biggest questions still unanswered?

The GE Capital Model of Integration[109]

Of course the exercise above is just one link in a long chain of merger integration. What are the other links? There are some important best practices to emulate. Take General Electric. Between 1993 and 1998 alone, GE Capital integrated more than a hundred mergers, increasing its workforce by 30 percent, globalizing its business, and doubling its net income. What were the key success factors? There were at least two. First, GE saw integration management as a separate business function, just like operations, marketing or finance. Second, the company sought to address cultural issues head-on by using "Cultural

Workouts" managed by outside facilitators to speed up integration and foster understanding of the partner company's culture.

The GE Capital model of integration includes seven steps that its managers take whenever the firm merges with another.

One, they look at integration as a process—not as a science but as an art. Even though there are predictable elements, we will never fully understand what it takes to work with other human beings, let alone to become one with another company.

Two, they make use of cultural assessment tools. The executives meet for several days, usually with an outside consultant, and identify the cultural barriers the merging entities face.

Three, they regard integration as a full-time job, and they allocate one manager to monitor the integration effort full-time until it is complete and all the post-merger pains (and wounds) have healed.

Four, they use urgency to catalyze immediate results by designing and launching a *catalytic project* for the teams of both merging parties to work on together. Catalytic projects are small-scale, short-term projects—usually lasting no more than a hundred days—teams carry out in order to test key assumptions about the merger in a "laboratory of action." Such projects should be both low-risk and low-cost so they don't sink the boat in case of failure. In case of success they can serve as proof-of-principle projects or path-breaking projects that alter the landscape of what is possible. There are several advantages in using a catalytic project: the teams can learn how to work together in an environment that is easy to control, any breakdowns can be resolved right away, and producing immediate results gives people a sense of success and boosts morale.

Five, they recognize that it is essential to communicate, communicate, communicate. You should never assume anything. You have to communicate decisively, fully, and instantaneously if there is any possibility of a misunderstanding or mistrust.

Six, they use three-day cultural workouts to train people in multi-cultural skills. The purpose of these sessions is for people of both sides to understand each other. They learn about each other's history and culture, the war stories of each company, what people are proud of, and what they do not like about their company. In this way, they build relationship, partnership, and trust. The cultural workout is usually scheduled for the last three days of the one-hundred-day project. It forges the two companies as a team. On the last day, they create their common future. They create a vision, a strategy, and the actions they will take together in the future.

Finally, they use a facilitator or coach. This could be a coach from within one of the merging companies, but it usually works better for both parties if the facilitator is outside the two cultures. That way he or she can bring a fresh point of view and see more impartially what drives people from both companies and what their cultural blind spots are.

In sum, a possible framework for cross-cultural integration is the "5C Integration Model," including Courtship, Confidentiality, Cultural Compatibility, Communication, and Completion.[110] Whatever the model is, the bottom line is this: if merging companies take GE's best practices to heart and do the Cultural Workout right, it alleviates post-merger pains, makes life easier for all concerned, maximizes synergistic performance, and ultimately saves the M&A from going awry. In a global bank that was having trouble integrating its private banking and investment banking operations after multiple mergers, the private bankers (although of course they did not admit this) tended to be more conservative, straight-laced, hierarchical, and risk-averse. The investment banking culture on the other side was much more freewheeling, testosterone-driven, participatory, and ad-hoc. Once the senior executives from each side took the point of view of the other side and were able to be in the other side's world, however, they were able to come up with operating principles and rules—what to do or not to do—that worked in interacting with the other side and laid the foundation for extraordinary joint performance.

Chapter Ten

Making Global Meetings Work

The meeting of two personalities is like the contact of two chemical substances; if there is any reaction, both are transformed.

Carl Gustav Jung

A Coca-Cola salesman returned from his assignment in Israel completely dejected. One of his colleagues asked him, "Why weren't you successful with the Israelis?" The salesman explained: "When I got assigned, I was very confident that I would make a good sales pitch. But, I had a problem. I don't speak Hebrew. So I planned to convey the message through these three posters:

First poster: a man lying in the hot desert sand, totally exhausted, fainting. Second poster: the man is drinking Coca-Cola. Third poster: our man is totally refreshed. These posters were widely distributed and seen by thousands.

"Then that should have worked!" said the friend.

"The hell it should have!" said the salesman. "I didn't know that they read from right to left!"

The focus of this final chapter is how to create, lead, and debrief meetings effectively when the people on your team are spread out in different parts of the world. By "effectively" I mean that the meetings produce the results you want, that they enable co-creation and ownership, and that they result in alignment among the participants. In other words, the experience of a true partnership and team rather than participants being reduced to mere recipients, or feeling that the meeting or teleconference is a fait accompli and that—all too often the reality—the corporate hierarchy is imposing the solutions on them without choice or co-creation.

Traditional vs. Virtual Meetings

First you have to be cognizant of the difference between face-to-face sessions (where you meet your colleagues across the table) and virtual meetings (a global conference call, a Skype call, or a videoconference). How do you choose the right medium?

First, in the traditional meeting you have much more cultural cohesion. You sit face to face and there is a sense of familiarity. When participants sit across the room, this leaves much less room for misunderstanding. When you say something, you can read your listeners' body language and see whether they understand what you are saying. When you speak to people over a TV or Skype screen or over the phone, you cannot tell easily whether they followed what you said. This structural impediment makes room for confusion—meanings get lost in translation.

Second, in traditional meetings, there is perceived equality. When you and I sit across from each other, we sit at the same table, so it does not feel hierarchical, even when I speak and you don't; you could respond at any moment. But when I speak at a teleconference in New York and mute your line in Helsinki, you probably perceive some inequality. I am in charge, I run the meeting, I send the signals and you don't really have a choice but to receive them (unless you hang up and are prepared to bear the consequences). This might lead to a certain recipient mentality on your part. You might feel that I am imposing my way of doing things on you—which is often not far from the reality.

The third difference is social context. In a face-to-face session, participants share social interaction and informality. We can crack jokes and be reasonably sure that our listeners will get the humor. I can ask something informally, I can whisper to you, I can drop somebody a note on the side. By contrast, the virtual session tends to be more official, which can lead to more formal interactions and diplomatic language. And that makes it much harder to have the grease of relationship, social interaction, and humor.

Finally, in the traditional meeting, you likely interact with people with whom you have had a background of shared relationship and shared practices for some time. You feel at home, your culture has become cohesive. In the virtual meeting, it is much more difficult: you are flying blind, and any ethnocentrism, real or perceived, is revealed in a harsh light. You can no longer rely on the fact that what you say will be understood. You might be unaware that your own cultural examples are not speaking to the other culture at all. An example of that are U.S. managers who use sports analogies like "the whole nine yards" or "move it down the field" or "let's kick their butt." Such statements may not be understood in another culture. So when you use sports analogies, you may want to use analogies of universal sports like tennis, which people understand in Germany ever since Boris Becker, or soccer rather than football if you speak to Brazilians or Europeans. Alternatively, you might use a set of analogies that come from a global background so that any human being can understand, such as war analogies (but note that they may be inappropriate in Nordic countries!) or Chinese proverbs.

How you communicate with colleagues spread out around the world is a strategic choice. Although virtual meetings are becoming the preferred way for keeping the global team in communication, they are not the only way. Traditional meetings still have their place. Let us look briefly at the advantages and disadvantages of virtual and traditional meetings.

The traditional meeting is the most expensive way for a global team to meet, so it will probably be used relatively rarely, especially in times of cost-cutting, since it is both travel- and time-intensive. Flying people from India to New York or London or vice versa is costly and takes valuable time. A two-day meeting in another country can easily consume a week when you include preparation, packing, travel, and jetlag. The opportunity costs can be enormous. Because of the high cost, the traditional meeting will not only happen less often, but also include fewer participants—usually just the key selected leaders of the organization.

Because it is less costly, a conference call or multi-point videoconference allows you to work with more people at one time and you can meet more frequently via video- or teleconferencing than in person. I have led videoconferences with more than 250 people and teleconferences with more than 1,000, at a lower cost than holding a global meeting with twenty people in New York.

Some have reservations about videoconferences as a communication medium. On a videoconference discussing this topic, one U.S. executive told me that in his company it was virtually unimaginable that their Mexican colleagues would attend because "the Mexicans just don't like videoconferences." But that belief is outdated. The question is, why were the Mexicans reluctant to use videoconferences? Is it that they never felt permission to shape the agenda and were constantly relegated to the receiving end? Is it that they felt imposed upon by the U.S. colleagues? I suggested that the executive rotate the leadership of the videoconferences and invite his Mexican colleagues to lead some of them.

The traditional meeting lends itself to macro management, where you deal with strategic or major policy issues. The virtual meeting lends itself to hands-on management, where you roll up your sleeves and get to work on the tactics.

You may want to create an annual schedule with a smart mix of traditional and virtual meetings. You could do so in a videoconference with all your key global team members. Talk about how often you should have traditional meetings. Do you fly everybody to a global face-to-face only once a year or once every quarter? At the same time that you discuss when to have these meetings, also decide where to hold them. See if you can meet not in the same but in different locations around the world. That allows the members of your team to enhance their ownership of the organization when they host their colleagues, and to learn more from one another and about their opportunities and people when they visit each other's locations. Articulate the purpose of both your in-person and virtual meetings, then decide who should attend them to fulfill that purpose.

Before: Co-Creating the Agenda

Like any meeting, a multicultural meeting is only as good as its preparation. You will have the gathering you prepare for and that you prepare each participant for. If you want to forge alignment at a meeting, you better cause the conditions for such alignment in the minds of a critical mass of participants beforehand. Here are a few ground rules that have worked in the companies I have served.

First, see the virtual meeting as a step in a process. Look at it not as an isolated event or a nice-to-have activity, but as an integral part of your company strategy for unleashing leadership.

Second, stand in the shoes of every participant. What are people's intentions, what are their concerns, what are their dreams? With one foot in their reality and one foot in their future, see the world from their perspective. What might matter to Alexandre right now? What do the Singaporeans need, given their objectives and current performance?

Third, co-create the purpose, intended results, and agenda of the meeting. As much as possible, design the meeting with the people who will be participating. It works when you send a draft agenda to all participants before the meeting (make sure to call it a "draft" so they don't feel it is cast in stone). It works when they know the intended outcomes and agenda beforehand. It works even better when you ask participants what they think about the meeting design.

Fourth, pay attention to all participants' local time zones and local customs. If at all possible, schedule the meeting so that it occurs during work hours for all participants—or at least so that it's not in the middle of the night in Melbourne or on a national holiday in Venezuela.

Fifth, experiment with rotating the meeting leadership. If you have participants in Bucharest, Berlin, and Buenos Aires, let someone from each location facilitate the meeting periodically. This will have the added benefit that you can really lead and are not constrained by the demands of being the moderator.

During: Keeping Things on Track

When you open the virtual meeting, say "Good morning, good afternoon, and good evening," or whatever the appropriate welcome would be given the locations and time zones of the participants. Be aware of the season in the parts of the world from which your participants are attending. A global teleconference can easily include New Yorkers who have battled a snowstorm to get to work and Argentineans who are leaving on their summer vacation the next weekend. Paying attention to such details will give participants the experience that you are "glocal"— meaning that you don't merely think global, act local but think local and act global.

It bears repeating: be sensitive that participants will have varying levels of proficiency with the language of the meeting. My colleague Shideh Bina has a practice for meetings that she conducts in English when English is not the first language of most of the attendees, particularly if she is in a non-English-speaking country. She begins by thanking the attendees for their generosity in allowing her to facilitate a meeting in English and apologizes for not speaking the home language in their country. She reports that every time she did that in the last 20 years, the meeting attendees visibly relaxed and the relationship with her grew significantly. I use a similar practice of asking the participants to raise their hands if English is not their first language; then I ask people to keep their hands raised and tell me which is their first language. I then say that I might sound like Arnold Schwarzenegger, and that they should feel free to stop me at any moment when my words don't make sense to them. It is a nice way to connect with the different cultures in the room and putting people on notice that their culture or way of doing business is not the only one.

Lead from the big picture, from your vision. Use the teleconference not for merely exchanging information, but for co-creation of a shared vision and strategy. Don't let details get in the way of accomplishing your purpose and intended results. Human beings seem to be hardwired to get easily distracted by operational details. If a micro issue shows up during the meeting, get it handled off-line or create a task force to deal with it after the meeting.

Speak and listen to every person as the key to the meeting and, more importantly, the future. Whether it is the company's president or the receptionist, that person is the key to the success of the conference. So treat each and every person in the meeting that way.

It helps to use a dose of understatement and self-deprecating humor when you address a global audience. One example of this is Tim Melville-Ross, the director general of the British Institute of Directors, who opened his speech to the institute's 1998 annual convention with these words:

It is a real pleasure to speak to such a large and distinguished audience. If you will forgive me just a moment's conceit, it at least shows that in this respect my career has not been without progress. The first ever speech I made was in a village hall on a filthy February evening. It was cold, the wind was blowing, the snow was falling and there was just one other person present. I felt I owed it to the fellow to go ahead, so I made my speech and he applauded politely and I left the platform, put on my coat and was about to depart when I felt a hand on my shoulder. He said to me: "Please don't go—I'm the next speaker!" Thank you all for being here.

After: Leveraging the Momentum

Complete the meeting by acknowledging everyone who made a key contribution to its success, including the agenda team, presenters, production people, and those who produced materials.

Debrief the meeting, both alone and with your agenda team. Ask these questions:

- Did we accomplish the purpose of the meeting?
- Which intended results did we achieve, and which not (and what is next in achieving the results we missed)?
- What worked and should be done again in the future, and what did not work and should be avoided?
- What promises and requests were made at the meeting, and who needs to be reminded or followed up with?
- What, if anything, is incomplete for any of the participants?
- What about the meeting should or could be communicated to people who did not attend—how can they be empowered with the results or shared understanding of the meeting?
- And finally, what is next to keep up the momentum from the meeting?

These ground rules go not only for global meetings or videoconferences, but for all communication vehicles from brochures to memos to a Web site. Take Web sites: since the Internet has no boundaries, how do you create a site that can communicate as effectively to someone in New Delhi as it does to someone in New York? Very few online platforms are truly global. The issue is not merely a matter of translating the words into different languages. Something seen as hip in Silicon Valley may not communicate to people in London, much less to browsers in Rome or Moscow. Every time you miss the culture of an audience, you miss an opportunity.

To build a global web site, use truly global focus groups. Include people from France or Japan or Brazil or South Africa, make it representative of all the regions of the world where you expect to have a significant market. Then find out if the focus group members understand all the facets of your site and if they find any features confusing or off-putting. See if the site gets the response you intend to generate

Case: $40 Million Value-Add from Cross-Cultural Strategy and Leadership

Let me close the chapter—and the book—with an example of what can happen when you transform an intercultural team's leadership capacity. A well-known medical device company had almost single-handedly created the market for contact lenses. Then came the meager years when the company fell behind the competition, all the way down to the #4 spot.

To turn the business around the company recruited a new chief executive, who soon hired Insigniam to help improve speed to market, enhance innovation, and cultivate a robust new product pipeline.

My colleagues began with a cultural assessment, which soon revealed the root cause: a risk-averse, slow moving, non-collaborative, hierarchical context. The R&D team moved new developments through the pipeline too slowly, and the business unit's culture hindered people from generating new products rapidly.

Worse, R&D and other departments, especially manufacturing and marketing, barely communicated. In fact, even team members who worked in the same department had different views on how the existing product development process worked, a surefire sign that the process wasn't working at all. The unsurprising result: the company was not developing products consumers needed or asked for if it even developed products at all—the last one had been stuck in the pipeline for *eight years.*

The new CEO moved quickly. He assembled the twenty-six leaders from across the company and from multiple cultures: France, India, Italy, Thailand, the United Kingdom, and the United States. In a series of work sessions they got together to build a shared understanding, a common vision and strategy, and the global leadership capacity to make it happen. The key leaders participated in a series of three-day workshops as part of a "High Performance Leader" program focusing on strategy design and execution. But first the leaders distinguished what it means to be an authentic leader and designed a new cultural context that was collaborative, innovative, and rapid.

At the end of the first work session, the participants took on several projects to each generate a breakthrough in their area of accountability. The consultants worked with the team to build a new process that would deliver five new breakthrough projects. Simultaneously, they brought high performance leadership development programming across geographies and functions to elevate leadership capabilities across the organization.

Previously the company had developed a single new product every two to three years. The new process enabled them to deliver five new products in a record time of 18 months from ideation to post-launch. At the end of the engagement, three products had been launched and fifteen new ones were in the pipeline. The company estimated the value-add at $40 million, equivalent to an approximate 9,900 percent ROI—on a relatively modest investment in the business unit's intercultural leadership and capacity. What is possible if we invest in global citizenship?

The Bottom Line

- Companies lose enormous amounts of money because they fail to invest in their global competencies. (Coca-Cola, Microsoft, and DaimlerChrysler lost billions in sales because of cross-cultural blindness.) These losses—through post-merger pains, missed opportunities, lawsuits, brain drain etc.—are preventable through early and relatively low-cost investment.

- Managers tend to commit one or several of Ten Capital Sins: 1. They think that the world plays by their rules. 2. They continue doing what they always did in the past. 3. They take English for granted. 4. They don't respect the cultural pathways for making things happen. 5. They don't stand in their hosts' shoes. 6. They forget to invest in relationships. 7. They jump from vision to action, forgetting about strategy. 8. They take the village by storm. 9. They choose the wrong people for overseas assignments. 10. They forget that their advice is heard as mere noise unless they create demand for that advice.

- Globalization is a synergy of (a) the rise of the BRICS (Brazil, Russia, India, China, and, most recently, South Africa) as economic powerhouses; (b) the shrinking of communication and transportation costs, the growth of international migration, and the emergence of the virtual team; (c) the rise of capitalism, the rise of global media (including social media like Facebook, LinkedIn, and Twitter—or their European and Asian cousins Xing, Viadeo, and Renren) and the Americanization of global culture; (d) the rise of international organizations and multinational corporations, and the end of industry specificity.

- Together, these factors have utterly transformed the landscape of how managers must go about working, producing results, and leading across borders. Under hyper-globalization, all entrepreneurs and managers must be global citizens. More important than knowing what gifts to bring to dinner in Singapore or how tobow correctly in Japan, they need to be competent at working with, persuading, and empowering people from totally different value systems.

- Managers can use four tools to prevent culture clash: Global Citizenship Do's and Taboos (a set of generic ground rules), the Onion Model (to get to the drivers of the target culture), the Global Integrator™ (to quickly anticipate and prevent possible culture clashes), and the Global Leader Pyramid™ (to work effectively with one or multiple target cultures).

- Traditional multinationals think they know what is best for the world. They radiate their products, strategies, and policies out into the world. But since innovation often comes not from headquarters but from far-flung peripheral markets, a new type of global corporation has arisen. Metanationals have the capacity to listen worldwide for best practices and new ideas.

- In mergers, acquisitions, alliances, or joint ventures, the key things managers can do is to communicate their expectations clearly, to stand in the shoes of the other side and see the world from the other party's vantage point, and to look at cultural integration as an ongoing and separate business process, just like operations, marketing, or finance.

- Global meetings differ fundamentally from local, culturally cohesive meetings, and face-to-face meetings differ from virtual meetings. For example, cracking the usual jokes or using sports analogies from your home culture will likely lead to misunderstandings and raised eyebrows (unless of course it is a self-deprecating joke!). You can either make or break your global partners by how you prepare, deliver, and debrief global meetings and teleconferences to build partnership, alignment, and common visions and strategies that lead to breakthroughs in performance.

Appendix

Daily Living Checklist

Being a global citizen includes, of course, not only knowing a target business culture but also the daily living in that culture. Unless you have items like food, housing, schools, entertaining, money, and health under control, they can trip you up and derail your business imperatives. Here is a sample of a daily living checklist for Geneva, Switzerland. Note that some of the information might have changed—this checklist is for illustration only.

- **Climate:** Temperate, -2° Celsius in January, 25° Celsius in July. 51–99 cm rain.
- **Hours:** e.g., Manor shopping center: Mon-Wed 9-19h, Thu 9-21h, Fri 9-1930h, Sat 830-18h, Sun closed.
- **Safety:** Watch out for drug areas or attacks (e.g., near the lake). Otherwise safe.
- **Shopping centers** (where to buy household, apparel, and pharmacy items): Rue du Marché. Expensive: Rue du Rhône (Globus, boutiques). Reasonable: Rue du Cornavin (Manor).
- **Grocery shopping** (type of food, when in season, where to buy, how to store): Best food quality in the world. All foods available. Migros (one of two biggest chains, founded by Gottlieb Duttweiler, a hero in Switzerland, who was famously unwilling to sell alcohol or cigarettes). Migros at the train station is open weekends.
- **Healthcare** (emergency, doctors, pharmacy): Check if your company pays for healthcare. Swiss healthcare is one of the best. Just go. #144 = emergency doctor (weekends). Fire #118, Police #117.
- **Insurance:** 0.7% of your salary is deducted by your employer for non-work or accident insurance. For example, Google reportedly pays its employees CHF 300/month for

their own insurance. Insurance premiums are not dependent on your income (unlike in other countries). A good
insurance advisor (independent, impartial) is
VermögensZentrum in Zurich.

- **Parks and recreation:** Public beaches (Genève Plage,
  Bains des Pâquis). Skiing paradise (downhill and cross-
  country, close to Verbier, Crans-Montana). Hiking paradise.
  Gyms (lifting weights). Rowing, kayak.

- **Education:** Best system: university, IMD Lausanne, School
  of Diplomacy & International Relations, Hospitality
  Management School Lausanne. Migros courses for language studies or continuing education.

- **Housing and utilities:** Use colleagues, personal contacts.
  Le Temps, Tribune de Geneve. There are selected auctions of
  real estate in wealthy areas, published in newspapers, and
  going to the highest bidder.

- **Transportation:** Airport: Geneva Cointrin. Train to city in six
  minutes. Traffic tends to be congested. Taxis are expensive
  and hard to find (and may not take children/babies). Use public transportation (trains, tram, bus), even if you go skiing.
  Trains are fantastic. If you get a car, you may need a permit.

- **Banking/Postal service:** Nothing on Sunday. Weekdays
  8am–4pm, maybe closed at noon. You may want to set up a
  PostFinance account, where account and transaction fees
  are very low.

- **Don't forget:** Clothing for all four seasons. Plugs, trans-
  former (220V).

The Intercultural Business Cycle

- Selection: Screening, Interviews, (Self-)Assessment,
  Executive Summary

- Qualification: 360° Interviews, Feedback, Executive
  Summary

- Preparation: Global Citizen Bootcamp (cross-cultural workshop pre-assignment, catalytic project, Global Leader work-shop or teleconference during assignment)

- Assignment/Culture Shock: Performance-based coaching (during assignment/during catalytic project to cause strategic results in the target culture)

- Re-Entry/Repatriation: Prepare/coach executive for and during re-entry

- Reintegration/Evaluation: Debriefing, Lessons Learned, Best Practices, Innovation, Leadership Coaching

Where Does It Hurt?

Ethnocentrism: The company's international people don't understand or deal effectively with their counterparts in target cultures.

Ambiguity: Cross-cultural managers don't know how to walk the fine line of respecting local customs and still getting the job done in other cultures.

Misunderstandings: People don't speak the same language; market opportunities and customers are lost in translation.

Cultural clashes: Global teams—and their results—suffer from clashing values, in-fighting, or lack of alignment.

Silo thinking: Walls between national offices or departments block the free flow of information or best practices.

Global Citizen Coaching

Screens expat candidates and matches the right people with the right assignments.

- Prepares managers (and families as needed) to parachute into any target culture and get the job done while respecting local customs.

- Helps managers avoid costly mistakes when working across borders.

- Helps reintegrate returning expats while enhancing innovation through global best practices.
- Helps organizations develop global leadership assets and/or aligned high-performance teams.

Culture Clash Bootcamp (Standard Outline)

Day 1:

- Worst practices: the DaimlerChrysler case
- Self-assessment: your cross-cultural IQ?
- Key cross-cultural relationships & issues
- The Global Integrator™: assessing cross-cultural gaps and culture clashes along eight dimensions of culture
- What is culture? The Onion Model
- The Global Leader Pyramid™: effective cross-cultural leadership and communication

Day 2:

- Debrief and lessons learned
- Best practices: "Metanationals"
- 100-Day Catalytic Projects
- Working as a global championship team
- Running global meetings and teleconferences smoothly and successfully

Notes

1 See http://www.snopes.com/travel/foreign/service.asp. Comedian Shelley Berman claims that this "dialogue never actually took place in any hotel anywhere in the world."

2 Albert Mehrabian. 1972. *Silent Messages: Implicit Communication of Emotions and Attitudes.* Independence, KY: Wadsworth Publishing.

3 http://www.kultur-und-management.com/artikel1.pdf

4 http://aibse.homestead.com/documents/07Rottig.pdf

5 Peter Drucker, "Management's New Paradigms," *Forbes,* October 5, 1998. 152–78.

6 This story may be a hoax, although Mike McConnell, U.S. Director of National Intelligence, claimed it was true in a speech to Johns Hopkins University's Foreign Affairs Symposium in March 2008: "I was in the signals intelligence business where you listen to the people talk and so on. This is true. It's an actual recording."

7 *Sydney Morning Herald.* October, 1, 2001.

8 *The Washington Post,* February 18, 2007.

9 Internet World Stats, "Top Ten Languages Used in the Web," http://www.internetworldstats.com/stats7.htm.

10 http://www.translated.net/en/languages-that-matter

11 *New York Times,* January 2, 2012.

12 Playwright Jim Sherman wrote this after Hu Jintao was named chief of the Communist Party in China. See http://www.ma.huji.ac.il/hart/humor/hu.html

13 I owe these examples to Windham International, now GMAC, and to the *Wall Street Journal.*

14 "ATC@JFK - Air China 981 (by Aldo Benitez)," http://www.youtube.com/watch?v=iWDElvjwaFU

15 *New York Times,* May 21, 2012.

16 World Economic Forum, "The Global Competitiveness Index, 2011-2012 Rankings," 2011.

17 *New York Times,* June 30, 1999.

18 *New York Times,* December 6, 1998.

19 Interview in *Spiegel,* March, 1999.

20 *Fortune,* November 22, 1999.

21 *Fortune,* July 17, 2007.

22 Jerry Seinfeld, "Comedian," documentary.

23 *New York Times,* May 17, 2000; J. Stewart Black and Hal B. Gregerson, "The Right Way to Manage Expats," Harvard Business Review, March 1999.

24 http://www.fsa.ulaval.ca/personnel/vernag/REF/Textes/Vermond.htm

25 Rebecca West. *Black Lamb and Gray Falcon: A Journey Through Yugoslavia.* London: Penguin, 1941, 2.

26 Peter Drucker, "Management's New Paradigms," *Forbes,* October 5, 1998. 152-78.

27 *Forbes,* September 5, 2011.

28 *New York Times,* September 15, 2011.

29 Shaun Rein, "What Coca-Cola Did Wrong, and Right, in China," *Forbes,* March 24, 2009.

30 http://www.ibtimes.com/articles/363408/20120716/coca-cola-company-ko-2q-earnings-preview.htm

31 *New York Times,* March 8, 2012.

32 http://www.tata.com/htm/Group_MnA_CompanyWise.htm

33 *New York Times,* September 28 ,2011.

34 *New York Times,* February 16, 2012.

35 *Bloomberg News,* September 1, 2011.

36 Antoine van Agtmael, *The Emerging Markets Century: How a New Breed of World-Class Companies is Overtaking the World.* New York 2007: Free Press. 13.

37 *Sunday Times,* January 29, 2012.

38 *Forbes,* March 8 and 9, 2011.

39 http://www.itu.int/ITU-D/ict/statistics/at_glance/KeyTelecom.html

40 10th annual Human *Development Report.* 1999. New York: UN Development Programme.

41 *New York Times,* March 21, 2001.

42 "Indian Outsourcing Companies Think Strategy Even as Pressure Mounts," IndiaKnowledge@Wharton, 16 December 2010. http://knowledge.wharton.upenn.edu/india/article.cfm?articleid=4552

43 Stephen Castles and Mark J. Miller, *The Age of Migration: International Population Movements in the Modern World.* New York 1993: The Guilford Press, 2–3; The World Bank, "Migration and Remittances," http://web.worldbank.org/WBSITE/EXTERNAL/TOPICS/0,,contentMDK: 21924020~pagePK:5105988~piPK:360975~theSitePK:214971,00.html

44 *New York Times,* April 28, 2012.

45 Adrian Bautista, "So Where's Home? A Film About Third Culture Kid Identity," video, Georgetown University, 2012. http://vimeo.com/41264088

46 *New York Times,* September 7, 2011.

47 http://money.cnn.com/magazines/fortune/fortune500/

48 *Forbes,* September 5, 2011.

49 *Wall Street Journal,* January 12, 2010.

50 Ryan Buddenhagen, "Varying Social Media Usage Across Cultures Will Impact ISEO and Marketing," January 10, 2012. http://www.webimax.com/blog/seo/varying-social-media-usage-across-cultures-will-impact-iseo-marketing-part-2

51 "25 US Mega Corporations: Where They Rank If They Were Countries," http://www.businessinsider.com/25-corporations-bigger-tan-countries-2011-6?op=1

52 *Forbes,* September 5, 2011.

53 C.K. Prahalad and Kenneth Lieberthal, "The End of Corporate Imperialism," *Harvard Business Review,* July–August 1998. 69-79.

54 *USA Today,* January 24, 2011.

55 *The Seattle Times,* December 8, 2008.

56 Benjamin Barber, *Jihad vs. McWorld: How Globalism and Tribalism are Reshaping the World.* New York 1995: Ballantine Books. 30.

57 C.K. Prahalad and Kenneth Lieberthal, *ibid.* 78.

58 World Trade Organization, Press Relaese, April 7, 2011.

59 Thomas D. Zweifel, *International Organizations and Democracy: Accountability, Politics and Power.* Boulder CO 2005: Lynne Rienner. 1.

60 One book that highlights the battle between globalization and tribalism is Benjamin Barber, *Jihad vs. McWorld: How globalism and tribalism are reshaping the world.* New York 1995: Ballantine.

61 *New York Times,* November 12, 2011.

62 *New York Times,* February 5, 2012.

63 I owe this joke to Lark van Hugo.

64 *New York Times,* November 16, 2011.

65 *New York Times,* May 22, 2012.

66 *New York Times,* February 5, 2012.

67 *New York Times,* October 11, 2011.

68 Mark Pagel. *Wired for Culture: Origins of the Human Social Mind.* New York 2012: W.W. Norton.

69 Lera Boroditsky, "Lost in Translation," *Wall Street Journal,* July 23, 2010.

70 *Ibid.*

71 *Ibid.*

72 Talmud, Pesahim 87b; see Hyman Goldin. *Ethics of the Fathers.* New York 1962: Hebrew Publishing Company. 10.

73 *Der Spiegel,* 52/2011.

74 Sources: United Nations, www.un.org ; The Global Hunger Project

Inc., www.thp.org ; Population Reference Bureau, *World Population Data Sheet,* www.prb.org.

75 http://www.wpf.org/reproductive_rights_article/facts

76 http://www.thp.org/learn_more/issues/women_children

77 http://en.wikipedia.org/wiki/List_of_countries_by_GDP_(nominal)_per_capita
source ^ See also http://www.imf.org/external/pubs/ft/weo/2012/01/weodata/index.aspx. Data refer mostly to 2011.

78 http://www.wri.org/publication/content/8373

79 http://www.un.org/geninfo/ir/index.asp?id=160

80 http://www.un.org/en/peacekeeping/operations/financing.shtml

81 http://www.sipri.org/media/pressreleases/milex

82 This concept has been going around the Internet. I am indebted to my friend Brenda Dash for making me aware of it. See also http://www.toby-ng.com/graphic-design/the-world-of-100/

83 Friedrich Huebler, "Trends in Adult Literacy, 1990-2008," http://huebler.blogspot.com/2010/09/lit.html

84 Adapted from "Ending Hunger Briefing," San Francisco *1985: The Hunger Project.*

85 Nisbett, Richard E., Kaiping Peng, Incheol Choi, and Ara Norenzayan, "Culture and Systems of Thought: Holistic vs. Analytic Cognition," *Psychological Review,* April 2001. Reviewed in *New York Times,* August 8, 2000.

86 I owe this joke to Michael Walleczek. See http://home.online.no/~gmorgan/jokes/pdf_files/Euro.pdf

87 I am grateful to Nicholas Wolfson for bringing this article to my attention. First published in the Arab Bulletin #60, August 20, 1917; reprinted in *Lawrence's Secret Dispatches from Arabia* (1937), 126-133; reprinted in part in Basil Liddell Hart, *T. E. Lawrence* (reprinted as *Lawrence of Arabia,* Da Capo Paperback, 1989), 142–147. The original manuscript is in the PRO/FO 882/7.

88 I owe these jokes to Peter Rosenwald, Lawrence Flynn, and Alan Koch.

89 Sathe, Vijay, "How do Decipher and Change Organizational Culture," in: R. H. Kilman and Associates, *Managing Corporate Cultures.* San Francisco 1985: Jossey-Bass.

90 Switzerland Constitution, adopted by Public Referendum April 18, 1999, in force since January 1, 2000, Preamble.

91 Michael Nugent, "America's Top Two Elected Officials," http://www.michaelnugent.com/best/americas-top-two-elected-atheists/

92 OECD Factbook, 2008. http://www.oecd-ilibrary.org/sites/factbook-

2010-en/03/01/01/index.html?contentType=/ns/StatisticalPublication,/ns/Chapter&itemId=/content/chapter/factbook-2010-24-en&containerItemId=/content/serial/18147364&accessItemIds=&mimeType=text/html

93 *New York Times,* April 7, 2012.

94 See Thomas D. Zweifel, *Leadership in 100 Days: A Systematic Self-Coaching Workbook.* New York 2010: iHorizon, for detailed tools for building each level of the Global Leader Pyramid™. http://www.thomaszweifel.com/Leadership_in_100_Days.html

95 *New York Times,* April 4, 2012.

96 Global Leader Pyramid Poster™. See http://www.thomaszweifel.com/The_poster.html

97 I owe this joke to Doris Hirsch. See http://www.monoculartimes.co.uk/politricks/french_intellectuals.shtml

98 Yves Doz, José Santos and Peter Williamson, *From Global to Metanational: How Companies Win in the Knowledge Economy,* Boston 2001: Harvard Business Review Press. 156, 176.

99 Lawrence M. Fisher, "Yves Doz: The Thought Leader Interview," *strategy + business,* 4th Quarter, 2002.

100 Shaun Rein, "What Coca-Cola Did Wrong, and Right, in China," *Forbes,* March 24, 2009.

101 *Ibid.*

102 Diane Brady, "Pepsi: Repairing a Poisoned Reputation in India," Bloomberg BusinessWeek, May 31, 2007.

103 http://www.kultur-und-management.com/artikel1.pdf

104 *New York Times,* December 19, 2011.

105 Michael Bonsignore, *Financial Times,* October 17, 2001.

106 Jovi Tañada Yam, "Enter: 'Super Mario'," *Business World Online,* November 15, 2001. http://itmatters.com.ph/column/yam_11222001.html

107 Alexa Fletcher, "Avoiding Post-Merger Blues," BearingPoint 2006.

108 Towers Perrin in co-operation with the Economist Intelligence Unit, *The role of human capital in M&A: A survey report based on the opinions of 132 senior executives worldwide.* Towers Perrin 2003.

109 This account is adapted from Ronald N. Ashkenas, Lawrence J. DeMonaco and Suzanne C. Francis, "Making the Deal Real: How GE Capital Integrates Acquisitions," *Harvard Business Review,* January–February 1998.

110 M. Beth Page, *Done Deal: Your Guide to Merger and Acquisition Integration,* 49–50.

Readings and Resources

My clients often ask me if we can suggest tools or resources that could help them be more effective in dealing with people from other cultures. This section is my response to those requests. All the instruments and publications that I recommend here will help you better understand and deal with different cultures and their people.

The key is to immerse yourself, immerse yourself, and then immerse yourself some more. If you are doing business with people from another culture, learn at least a little bit of their language. It goes a long way to establish trust if you can speak some French or Spanish or Mandarin. Read some books about that culture or by well-known authors from that culture. For instance, I suggest reading a novel by Thomas Mann if you want to do business in Germany or poems by Pablo Neruda to know more about Latin America. Read articles about the culture. If you don't like to read, watch movies from the target culture, particularly movies filmed in that country in the native language. Do an Internet search about the culture. What you want to do is to see the world from that culture's point of view.

Several publications will give you a better idea of the cultures of different countries. Two that stand out are *The Week* and the *World Press Review;* both summarize media coverage from around the world. Let's say you had a question about how Steve Jobs was perceived around the world, for example in China and Australia. You could read excerpts of Jobs' obituary in the Beijing *Express* and find out what the *Sydney Morning Herald* had to say. You get world coverage about any number of issues in every edition. So this is a very useful tool for allowing you to understand how people from other cultures think about particular business, economic, political, and social issues.

The *Economist Intelligence Unit* and the CIA's World Factbook both offer a series of country briefings that, in a few pages, give you a wealth of information on any country, including an overview of the culture, geography, history, economics, and politics. *EIU* also publishes a "Worldwide Cost of Living Survey." www.eiu.com or https://www.cia.gov/library/publi cations/the-world-factbook/geos/xx.html

If you wish to understand the underlying root causes of why people live and buy as they do, check out the work of my colleague Clotaire Rapaille on cultural archetypes. http://www. archetypediscoveriesworldwide.com/learn.html

If you do a lot of business in Europe, read *The Europeans,* a book by Luigi Barzini, an Italian journalist. It is a very entertaining book about culture. Even though it is about Europe, it gives you the tools for thinking about and decoding other cultures.

Another book series I recommend is *The Xenophobe's Guide to the . . .* Published by Ravette Publishing in the United Kingdom, it is a series of guidebooks, each on a particular culture, and each informative and entertaining.

Here is a list of books that I have found most useful in my own quest for global citizenship:

Axtell, Roger E. *The Do's and Taboos of Body Language Around the World.* John Wiley & Sons, 1998.

Barber, Benjamin. *Jihad vs. McWorld.* New York: HarperCollins, 1996.

Barzini, Luigi. *The Europeans.* Penguin, 1983.

Bate, J. Douglas and Johnston, Robert E. Jr. *The Power of Strategy Innovation.* New York: Amacom, 2007.

Borden, George A., Conaway, Wayne A., and Morrison, Terri. *Kiss, Bow or Shake Hands: How to Do Business in Sixty Countries.* Adams Media Corp, 1995.

CompuServe. *Getting Through Customs (GTC)* (database on 65 countries).

Friedman, Thomas. *The Lexus and the Olive Tree.* New York: HarperCollins, 2003.
The World Is Flat. A Brief History of the 21st Century. New York: Farrar Straus & Giroux, 2005.

Conaway, Wayne A., Douress, Joseph J. and Morrison, Terri. *Dun & Bradstreet's Guide to Doing Business Around the World.* Prentice Hall Press, 2000.

Handy, Charles. "Trust and the Virtual Organization." *Harvard Business Review,* May–June, 1995.

Heidegger, Martin. *On the Way to Language*. San Francisco: Harper & Row, 1971.

Lieberthal, Kenneth and Prahalad, C.K. "The End of Corporate Imperialism." *Harvard Business Review,* July–August, 1998, 69–79.

Lipnack, Jessica and Stamps, Jeffrey. *Virtual Teams: Reaching Across Space, Time, and Organizations with Technology*. New York: John Wiley & Sons, 1997.

Nichols, Michael P. *The Lost Art of Listening*. New York: Guilford Publications, 1995.

Ohmae, Kenichi. *The Borderless World: Power and Strategy in the Interlinked Economy*. New York: HarperCollins, 1990.

Parker, Philip M. Linguistic Cultures of the World. Westport CT: Greenwood Publishing Group, 1997.

Rapaille, Clotaire. *The Culture Code: An Ingenious Way of Understanding Why People Around the World Live and Buy as They Do*. New York: Broadway, 2006.

Schell, Michael and Solomon, Charlene Marmer. *Capitalizing on the Global Workforce: A Strategic Guide for Expatriate Management*. New York: McGraw-Hill, 1996.

Sen, Sondra. *Interacts*. 2001. Business culture briefings for forty countries. Available at www.swissconsultinggroup.com .

Tomb, Howard. *Wicked French for the Traveler*. New York: Workman Publishing, 1988.

Wicked German for the Traveler. New York: Workman Publishing, 1992.

Wicked Greek for the Traveler. New York: Workman Publishing, 1995.

Wicked Italian for the Traveler. New York: Workman Publishing, 1988.

Wicked Japanese for the Traveler. New York: Workman Publishing, 1991.

Wicked Spanish for the Traveler. New York: Workman Publishing, 1991.

Watzlawick, Paul. *Gebrauchsanweisung für Amerika*. München: Piper, 2000.

Zweifel, Thomas D. *Communicate or Die*. New York: SelectBooks, Inc., 2003.

International Organizations and Democracy: Accountability, Politics, Power. Boulder, CO: Lynne Rienner Publishers, 2005.

Leadership in 100 Days: A Systematic Self-Coaching Workbook. New York: iHorizon, 2010.

About the Author

Thomas D. Zweifel is a management consultant, leadership professor and author. With three decades in management and consulting, while living on four continents, he has helped senior executives at numerous Fortune 500 companies—as well as governments, UN agencies, the military and a football/soccer club—to build global strategy alignment, leadership, and high-performance organizations in the action of meeting strategic and/or breakthrough objectives. In 1997 he co-founded Swiss Consulting Group, which was named a "Fast Company" by *Fast Company* magazine. From 2011 through 2012 he worked closely with Insigniam, an international management consultancy whose clients have documented, in aggregate, more than 50x ROI in savings and business results by specializing in enterprise transformation, innovation, change management, and breakthrough performance. Today he is Partner and Managing Director at Manres AG, a boutique consultancy in Switzerland and Germany. His clients have achieved breakthrough results in the most diverse cultural environments, and often under adverse circumstances. Some results were:

- Facilitating senior European executives at a top-tier global energy company with 80 million customers to produce 1 more per customer in shops ($73 million additional revenue) while spreading a leadership and coaching culture across the organization.

- Assisting the senior IT management team at a global bank in building a shared vision and strategy for off-shoring 5,000 knowledge workers, establishing channels for open communication, and boosting morale while achieving $200 million in cost savings.

Since 2000 Dr. Zweifel has taught leadership at Columbia University, St. Gallen University, and business schools in Australia, Israel, Switzerland, and the United States.

He is the author of six books on leadership, including *Communicate or Die: Getting Results Through Speaking and Listening* (SelectBooks, 2003); *Leadership in 100 Days: A Systematic Self-Coaching Workbook* (iHorizon, 2010); and *The*

Rabbi and the CEO: The Ten Commandments for 21st Century Leaders (SelectBooks, 2008; with Aaron L. Raskin) which was short-listed for the National Jewish Book Award and Foreword Book of the Year. Strategies based on Dr. Zweifel's books are used by 30+ Fortune 500 companies, the U.S. State Department, the U.S. Military Academy at West Point, and government agencies in North America, Europe, and Asia.

Dr. Zweifel speaks English, German, French, and Italian. He holds a PhD in International Political Economy from New York University and often appears in the media, including ABC News, Bloomberg TV, and CNN. His interdisciplinary and action-packed keynotes have inspired audiences in Australia, Canada, France, Germany, India, Israel, Italy, Japan, Kazakhstan, Netherlands, Russia, Sweden, Switzerland, and the United States.

In 1996 he realized his dream of breaking three hours in the New York City Marathon and in 1997 was recognized as "the fastest CEO in the New York City Marathon" by the Wall Street Journal. After living for twenty-four years in Germany, India, Japan, the United Kingdom and the United States, he is now based in Zurich, where he lives with his wife and their two daughters.

Your toughest time ever?

When I lived and worked in India in 1987, I almost died of a double infection — bacterial and amebic at the same time. The doctor came and said: "You must go to the hospital." I said: "No, I have no time for this, I have work to do." He simply slapped me in the face and took me to Bombay Hospital. I was in a room with eight others, and all the religions of the world were represented in the room — Hindus and Buddhists and Catholics and Muslims, and there was wailing and praying night and day. A nurse sat next to my bed for nine days and nine nights. Along with losing almost all the water in my body, I hopefully lost some arrogance and gained some humility.

It took seven years to install a phone line while I lived in India. My task was to train fourteen local leaders to deliver a workshop across the nation. My efforts were frustrated at every turn. It was very, very hard, but I got the job done. As a consequence of our effort, millions of people have taken charge of their destiny and have uplifted themselves from the conditions of hunger.

Your worst job ever?

Once I was consulting an organization where no one listened to each other. It was almost physically painful to even be there. When people don't listen to each other, they jeopardize organizations.

Your greatest concern about the future?

Consumerism. One of my greatest fears is that we become passive, resigned, indifferent, self-centered individuals who have no interest in serving the community.

Your heroes?

Two leaders: Churchill, for embodying leadership and for reminding us that "We make a living by what we get, but we make a life by what we give." And Gandhi, whom Churchill called "that little naked man," for teaching us integrity. My favorite story about Gandhi is this:

Once, a mother traveled for many days—by train, by rickshaw, by bus, and by foot—to bring her young son to Mahatma Gandhi. She begged, "Please, Mahatma. Tell my son to stop eating sugar."

Gandhi was silent for a moment. He said, "Bring your son back in two weeks." The woman was puzzled, but she thanked him and said that she would do as he had asked. She traveled all the way back to her village.

Two weeks later, she undertook the entire trip again—train, rickshaw, bus, and foot—and returned with her son. When they stood before Gandhi again, he looked the youngster in the eye and said, "Stop eating sugar."

Grateful but bewildered, the woman asked, "Why did you tell me to bring him back in two weeks? You could have told him the same thing then."

Gandhi replied, "Two weeks ago, *I* was eating sugar."

More Books by Thomas D. Zweifel

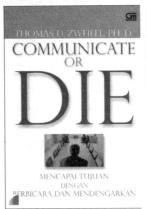

Communicate or Die: Getting Results Through Speaking and Listening. New York: SelectBooks. (Also in French, German, Indonesian, Chinese)

Culture Clash: Managing the Global High-Performance Team. New York: SelectBooks. (Also in French)

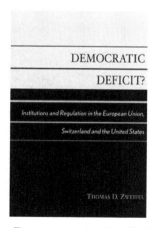

Democratic Deficit? Instituions and Regulation in the European Union, Switzerland and the United States.
Lanham MD: Lexington Books.

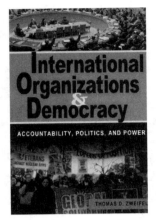

***International Organizations and Democracy:
Accountability, Politics, and Power.*** Boulder, CO:
Lynne Rienner Publishers.

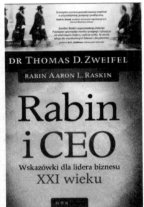

***The Rabbi and the CEO: The Ten Commandments for
21st Century Leaders.*** New York: SelectBooks. (Co-author
Aaron L. Raskin; National Jewish Book Award finalist,
Foreword Book of the Year Award finalist) (Also in German,
Polish)